Be Straight with Me

Andrews Mcmeel Publishing
a division of Andrews Mcmeel Universal
1130 Walnut Street, Kansas City, Missouri 64106

www.andrewsmcmeel.com

20 21 22 23 24 BVG 10 9 8 7 6 5 4 3 2 1

ISBN: 978-1-5248-5649-6

Library of Congress Control Number: 2020931551

ATTENTION: SCHOOLS AND BUSINESSES

Andrews McMeel books are available at quantity discounts with bulk purchase for educational, business, or sales promotional use. For information, please e-mail the Andrews McMeel Publishing Special Sales Department: specialsales@amuniversal.com.

Be Straight with Me

emily e. dalton

Andrews McMeel
PUBLISHING®

A NOTE ON THE TEXT

Memories—like reflections in a mirror—appear differently depending on who is looking. I have reflected on this story as honestly as possible and portrayed the events to the best of my memory.

Some names and identifying details have been changed to protect the privacy of the people involved.

This
book is
dedicated to
the understanding
that we all exist along
the same spectrum—
however far one end
may be from
the other.

But
mostly
to the ones
who are still afraid,
or misinformed,
or in denial about
what it means
to land
somewhere
in the middle.

Love is like the wild rose-briar,
Friendship like the holly-tree—
The holly is dark when the rose-briar blooms
But which will bloom most constantly?

— Emily Brontë, "Love and Friendship"

Either the well was very deep, or she fell very slowly,
for she had plenty of time as she went down to look about her
and to wonder what was going to happen next.

— Lewis Carroll, *Alice's Adventures in Wonderland*

SOPHOMORE SEPTEMBER

Your call echoes over a warm
end-of-summer breeze
that shakes the leafy branches
of the elms and maples
lining the sidewalk.

"Hey! You girls blaze?"

Joanna and I are trudging up
the big hill on College Street
on our way back to Milliken
after a brief stint at a house party.

The soccer team had blasted
Katy Perry songs and danced
around shirtless on their roof
until Public Safety yelled at them.

(At a small private college
like Middlebury,
you can get away with a lot
if you only
do a little
at a time).

Soggy half-smoked cigars were
disemboweling in the kitchen sink,
underclassmen were passed out
on chairs in the living room,
and everything was sticky.
We left fifteen minutes after arriving.

And now, your shadowed silhouette
grows larger as it approaches up the hill.
Broad shoulders, loose-fitting clothes,
and the swaggering gait of a young guy.

Mostly in shadow but vaguely familiar—
your round, lightly freckled face,
half of it covered in a short, thick beard,
the waves of dirty blond hair
under a black and red snapback.

Months later, I'll connect the dots . . .

how one night in the
winter of freshman year
we happened to be waiting
for the same campus shuttle
in the dark, cold vestibule
on Adirondack Circle.

It was me,
Dave from across the hall,
Dave's friend Douglas,
and you—

Max Willard.

We played Kill Fuck Marry,
and something about you
rubbed me the wrong way,
so I chose to kill you.

Little did I know that minutes earlier,
when Dave and Douglas and everyone else
had left the pregame in my room
to go catch the ride,
you'd lingered behind
and stolen a twenty-dollar bill off my desk,
because you saw me at a party once
and thought I looked like

"a snarly bitch."

But right now, I don't recognize you.
I have no idea
that your name is Max
or that you're the same year as me
or why the faint familiarity of your face is
giving me a tentative, queasy feeling.

I don't remember that
I once wanted you dead.

As you stand there in front of us,
your cuffed khakis clashing with your jean jacket
in a way that almost seems intentional,

the nearly full moon casts
a filter of gray light
over your skin,
giving you
a ghostly glow.

And I don't know it yet,
but every fall to come
will make me think of you.

REFLECTIONS: FIRST GRADE

I'm the youngest
and the only blonde
in a family of redheads.

"Now where did this one come from?"
"One of these is certainly not like the others!"

I know
I wasn't adopted
but sometimes
it feels that way.

SOPHOMORE SEPTEMBER, CONTINUED

Under the gray moonlight,
on the big hill on College Street,

you tell us you heard
that we like to smoke weed,
and you're always on
the lookout for
"chill girls who smoke weed."

Joanna invites you back to our dorm,
and as we walk, you and Jo go back
and forth naming people you know,
while I can't decide whether I feel
less awkward walking in silence
beside you or in front of you.

When we get to Milliken,
Bobby Garthon, a football bro
who lives down the hall,
is yelling drunkenly up
to a fifth-floor window.

He doesn't have any shoes on . . .
and I'm happy because
his strange presence
makes me feel less like the odd girl out.

"Never mind, fuckface!
Jo is here to save the day,"
he shouts up at the window,
slurring his words.

Bobby fist-bumps you,
decides he's going to join us,
and then falls asleep sitting up
on the end of Joanna's bed.

We're about to smoke
our miniature bong, Miss Cleo,
when you pull out a pipe
that looks like
     a grimy
   glass
dildo.

You call it the Steam Roller.
Which is appropriate,
because that's what you do
with your blunt confidence
as you take over our space
and ignore every word I try to say.

I open the window just to feel
like I'm contributing something.

You goad Bobby to wake up.
With a dopey smile on his face,
eyes closed, he goes, "Shh, shhh,"
and slumps his head on his shoulder.

"Wait," you say, "do you guys even know him?"
"He lives down the hall from us," I reply.
You don't respond to me.
You turn your attention to Joanna,
who asks in return how *you* know Bobby Garthon.

"Oh, me and Bobby-boy go way back."
You explain how you went to high school together
at an all-boys Catholic school.

"Sure did," you say, making an irreverent
sign of the cross. "The Lord is my shepherd."

Still, you aren't really talking to me—
more to Joanna—so I try to look
as bored with you
as you already seem to be
with me.

I know this has an effect because,
when I ask whether you were close with Bobby,
for the first time all night,
you actually look at me.

You share that you had only one friend
in high school, Pete,
and that Pete
was the only black kid
and you were the only gay kid.

You raise your eyebrows at me,
and I think you might have noticed
how that last bit of information
just caught me off guard.

Up until then, I couldn't really tell.

We smoke the Steam Roller some more,
Miss Cleo sits on my desk ignored,

and then it's time for you to go.
You begin belting out,

"Ri-ISE and shi-INE
and give God that glory, Garthy!"

Finally, Bobby opens his eyes.
He shakes his head like a wet dog
and follows you out of the room.

As I close the door behind you,
I hear you in the hallway
trying to get Bobby to harmonize with you,
singing,

"Our God is an awesome God!"

REFLECTIONS: FIFTH GRADE

The song "All the Things She Said" by t.A.T.u.
has everybody at school gossiping.
It's about two girls . . .
kissing.

My worst fears are confirmed:
girls *can* be gay.

FRIENDS BY DEFAULT

The next day, I walk into my room and find
you and Jo sprawled on the carpet
watching Major Lazer music videos.

Those first few weeks,
you and I tolerate each other
because we don't seem to have a choice.

You like Jo much more than you like me,
but I'm her roommate,
and you live all the way down
the big hill in the German House,
so you're always in our room.

By October, we're hanging out almost every day.
We're friends, I guess . . .

Still, we rarely spend time together
if Joanna isn't there.

You're starting to feel
like our third roommate,
but I'm still feeling

like the third wheel.

REFLECTIONS: SIXTH GRADE

Mom dries my hair
with a blow dryer,
my stupid blonde curls
burned away by hot air.

Now I feel girly and cute
for the family picture,
and at school,
everyone's telling me
that Steve Girard
has a crush on me!

YOU INVITE US TO WATCH THE *REAL WORLD*
PREMIERE

I'm not ready yet.
I just got out of the shower.
Joanna doesn't mind, but
you mock me in a nasally voice,

"I'm Emily, and I have wet hair and glasses."

You don't know that I hate my hair,
my unruly blonde frizz that needs straightening.

You don't know that I used to walk around campus
blind—barely able to see a friend's face ten feet away.
I was afraid to wear my glasses in public
and still hadn't learned how to put in my contacts.

But tonight I leave my dorm
with wet hair and glasses.

When we arrive at the watch party,
you settle into a spot on the floor
at the center of the room. There are
about twenty kids, all laughing and shouting
at the TV screen.

Someone hands you a bottle of tequila.
You open it with a huff of impatience.

I begin to notice that everyone
crammed in this small dorm room
is equally as absorbed by your

every move as they are
by the roommates claiming beds
in the *Real World* house.

In fact, everyone is here
much more for you
than for the show.

All of this comes together for me
as I sit here quietly on the edge of a bed
with Joanna, among dozens of your closest friends,
watching as they reach out and hug you
and shake your shoulder
and laugh with you.
I know this season of *The Real World*
is particularly significant at Middlebury
because someone who graduated last year is on it.

But I've forgotten
that you dated that someone—
Chris, the hot gay senior—
when we were freshmen.

Your first real boyfriend and
your first great heartbreak.

This crowded room of sophomores
is your own personal support group,
here to offer company, condolence, and tequila
as you watch your ex-boyfriend
go to clubs and parties and
hook up with random people
on reality television.

Sitting here in the corner
with my wet hair and glasses,
I look around the room
in envious awe.

These are the friends
who knew you last year,
the ones who accepted you
with open arms
when you came out to them.

They were there for you
during your first real relationship with a man
and your subsequent heartbreak,
all before I even knew you.

Every time Chris comes on-screen,
you take a pull from
the bottle of tequila,
and everyone laughs, and so do you,
but your eyes never leave the TV.

Toward the end of the episode,
Kayla, a girl with alopecia,
gets up to leave early for a night class.

She says her goodbyes.
As she steps over bodies on the floor,
you call out to her,

"Baldy! Are you leaving?"

For a moment, my brain and my ears debate,
Did he really just say that? How drunk is he?

My eyes dart to Kayla's face,
but she barely bats an eye,
laughing, making her way over to you
for a hug goodbye
as if you called her a name as benign as
"sweetie" or "honey."

No one seems concerned, and now
it's clear you call her this all the time.

Maybe you aren't spewing crude language
for the sake of entertainment.
Maybe you aren't penetrating insecurities
and crossing lines
just for a reaction.

Maybe you're pointing out our quirks—
the things that make us unique—
to help us own them . . .

All of us, piled on twin beds
and sprawled across the floor,
are here laughing and bonding because you decided
to own your very public heartbreak.

I'm sitting here with my wet hair and my glasses,
wondering whether there was an unspoken message
in your mockery of me earlier.

Perhaps,
when you teased me
what you meant was,

"I'm Emily, and I have wet hair and glasses . . .
and I foolishly think I'm less beautiful for it."

REFLECTIONS: NINTH GRADE

It's the first year of high school
and the first year
that I'm the last sibling
left in the house
alone
with Mom and Dad.

I dye my hair once
and then I can't stop:

bleach blonde
    yellow blonde
dirty blonde
    light brown
dark brown
        red
and all the muddled colors in between.

Just a few short hours
of lathering and rinsing,
a squirt of ammonia here,
a squeeze of hydrogen peroxide there . . .

and my roots disappear
beneath the exhilaration
of a new shade.

YOUR FRIENDS LIKE TO ASK

"How do you solve a problem like Max Willard?"

What is it about
your love for German and Maria von Trapp?

Your affinity for the bizarre phonics
of a language that compels you to shout things like
"*Das ist Quatsch!*" and "*schwieriges Leben*" at random?

Your knowledge of dance-club culture in Berlin?

Your fixation on a country
still healing from its tragic history
of identity-suppression
and shame?

I'll never tell you that sometimes,
when Jo and I sit with you and your friends
in the dining hall, or pregame with you
on the sixth floor of Milliken,
I confess to myself
that you fascinate me

with your shaggy, unkempt hair,
your grungy fashion sense,
and your posse of hot straight guy friends with whom you
shotgun beers and
smoke pot and
play Xbox.

(You have so many straight guy friends,
I think you must like to torture yourself.)

AND I DON'T LIKE TO ADMIT IT, BUT

you're funny,
and I admire your
shameless ability to speak your mind,
and I marvel and laugh at your nonsense
when you say things like:

"So who breastfeeds who around here?"
"Pinch my nips and call me a poodle!"
"Daddy's got a new pair of jeans!"

Or when you break an awkward silence with

"So what's everyone being for Halloween?"

. . . in the middle of April.

I'm having trouble determining whether
you fascinate me because I'm scared of you
or I'm scared of you because you fascinate me.

But also
I think I'm coming to realize
this is all just your way
of commanding order over the chaos,
keeping people at arm's length, and
holding your wildest cards
close to your chest.

Because how can anyone ever judge you
if they have no idea what you're saying?

REFLECTIONS: FOURTH GRADE

At soccer practice
Nicole and Kelsey and Lynn
talk about boys and kissing.

Will a boy ever want to kiss me?

Do I ever want to kiss a boy?

HALLOWEEN

You've known Joanna and me long enough now
to be well aware
that we are *not* the kind of girlfriends
who make out with each other.

Joanna and I are Harry and Lloyd from *Dumb and Dumber*.

I'm Harry in a big furry dog costume.
Joanna is Lloyd, dressed like a limo driver.

You're wearing a short red wig
over your dirty blond hair
and a deep shade of red lipstick that
makes your Cheshire grin pop
amidst your dark stubble.

You deepen your voice,
mocking the tone of a drunk jock.
"You ladies look pretty sexy in those costumes.
Dare you to make out."

I shiver off the burn of another shot of Jack Daniel's.
Joanna and I look to one another and roll our eyes.
We both know you could care less
about watching two girls make out.

"Why not?" you say.
"Is it because Dalton's a bad kisser?"
You smirk at me. I give you the finger.

"I'm probably a better kisser than you, Willard."

You stifle a laugh,
and I want to smack you.

"I just don't see you as the good kisser type," you say.
"I'm sure you're decent in your own way, though."

Now I'm really about to slap you, but Joanna intervenes.

"If you're both so good at it,
then I dare *you* two to make out!"

I expect you to mirror my disgust,
but a different expression comes over your face.
An expression of challenge.

I see that
this is not just your average make-out dare;
this is a duel of skill,
a showdown of sex appeal.

Here I can show you once and for all
I'm not just some oblivious bimbo.

I match your competitive glare
and utter one contemptuous, bored word of consent.

"Fine."

The next thing I know, we're horizontal
against my pillows, arms around each other,
accepting Joanna's deflected dare in full force.
Then, just as quickly as it seemed to happen,
it's over.

I sit up, fix the hood of my dog suit,
casually wipe your lipstick off my mouth.
You stand with a disinterested look on your face,
then go to the mirror on my desk.

"Did that mess up my lipstick?" you mumble to yourself.

Joanna lets out a burst of laughter.
"What was that?!" she shrieks.

We glance at one another, shrugging.
"Not bad," you say.
"I guess," I reply.

"Do you guys need me to leave?"
Joanna asks, still laughing at us
as we clink shot glasses
and throw our heads back in a gulp.

Then you crank the volume
on a Benny Benassi remix
and start dancing,
and the moment has passed.

REFLECTIONS: SECOND GRADE

Do I have a pretty face?
Is my hair long enough?

What do the pretty girls do?
Watch them closely . . .

JOANNA GETS A BOYFRIEND

Jo's new boyfriend has lots of money
and a fancy car and his own room.

Now there's an empty bed
across from mine
almost every night.

One evening in November,
as Jo's gathering her overnight bag,
you ask whether you can sleep in her bed—
you'd rather not make the long walk
back to the German House.

Jo suggests that it's really up to me.

I shrug over my homework,
wondering whether this means
you and I are actually friends.

Am I annoyed you assume I won't mind?
Or flattered
you're willing to spend
time alone with me?

The next morning, you tell me
I was talking in my sleep,
saying "Wow!" over and over.
Curious what was so impressive,
you tried to talk back until
you realized I was just dreaming.

You imitate my sleep-talking,
and we're both hysterically laughing,
and then I have this weird feeling like
I don't want to leave for class.

Each night after this,
we lie on opposite sides of the room,
you in Jo's bed, me in mine,
giggling back and forth through the dark
until we fall asleep.

We grow close, like siblings
in twin beds.

One morning, as I'm putting on makeup before class,
you roll over and ask, in a voice hoarse from sleep:
"Why do you have to wear that stuff all the time?"

"I don't have to . . . I just like to . . ." I respond.
"Look at me."
"What?"
"Just look at me for a second. Let me see," you insist.

When I look at you,
you roll onto your back,
close your eyes,
and pull the covers up.

"I think you look better without makeup,"
you say beneath the covers.
"And I'm not just saying that so you'll
turn the light off and let me sleep."

No one—especially no *male*—could actually think
I look better without my dark eye makeup.
It's like something my mom would say . . .

OKAY

On Sunday night after Thanksgiving break,
we're back on campus.

You point to the oversized get-well card hanging
over my bed. It's not new, but you haven't asked
me about it until now. So I tell you
about the time I wished
I was dead,

months before, in the summer,
during the bloody post-op complications
of a tonsillectomy gone terribly wrong.

I've never voiced this before.
Not since the night I said it out loud,
hunched over in the backseat
on the way to Hartford Hospital.
It was my third post-op bleed in less than a week.

As my father sped
through every red light in our path
and the crimson of blood-soaked tissues
grew deeper and darker inside the bucket on my lap,
I croaked out the words, to no one in particular,
"I want to die."

I kept my head down so the blood
wouldn't seep down the back of my throat
and drown me in it.

The blood congealed into chunks in my teeth
as the ER doctors cauterized the open wounds.
The scene was so gruesome that
my dad and sister had to leave the room;
they thought they might vomit.

I didn't want to drown in my own blood.
But I did want to die.

You listen quietly
as I open up to you.

Then, you don't ask me whether I'm okay;
you remind me that I am.

And you climb out of Joanna's bed
and lean down
to hug my horizontal body.

It's not one of those robotic
going-through-the-motions
types of hugs. It's real.
So real that I almost cry.
Then you're letting go
and crossing back through
the darkness to Joanna's bed.

And I really do feel okay.

REFLECTIONS: THIRD GRADE

At recess, a girl in my class
asks me about my sneakers
and tells me that

"They only have Sambas in the *boys'* section."

So, can I still wear my favorite shoes . . .

. . . even though they're meant for boys?

GIRL TALK

We're partying at the Bunker—
the old concrete building on the edge of campus,
once a dining hall, now notorious
for its epic dance parties—
when I first spot George Dale.

He's wearing these white leather bejeweled
cowboy boots (in an ironic way, I presume),
and I just *have* to ask him about them.

He's cute and funny, and, oh,
he lives in the same building as me . . .

We have a series of drunk sleepovers
interspersed with a few unplanned,
slightly awkward meals in the dining hall.

One morning, you come into the room
to get Miss Cleo, and I'm under the covers
with George, and you make a stupid face
and ask, "Are you guys naked?"

By winter, George starts
to distance himself from me.
And even though you tell me not to,
I confront him drunkenly
at an off-campus party.

I get an explanation that makes
zero sense. I want to scream
and find you
and leave this stupid party.

But you might have already left,
and you're not texting me back.

The following afternoon,
I come into my room
and you're already there,
sitting on the flowery rug.

(Is it weird that there's
something I really love about
how comfortable you are
hanging out in my room
alone, as if it's yours?)

I heave a sigh about that stupid freshman, George Dale.
"He thinks I smoke too much pot!
He thinks I'm too big of a stoner!"

You're laughing,
and now I'm trying not to laugh
as you point out that George Dale smokes
just as much as I do.

"He said it's different 'cause I'm a girl.
He said it's weird that I'm a girl
who smokes more than he does."

You snort, and you're right.
I don't even like him that much,

and, yes, he is kind of hot, but
he's also kind of a freak . . .
which is why it pisses me off so much!
In the beginning, he was like,
"Oh, Emily, you're so cool;
you're so different from other girls,"
and then, *"Oh, you're not*
a normal-enough girl."

You tell me to get over it.
I know you're right, but whatever.

"Did you really think he was hot, though?" I ask.
You shrug. "I would say he was cute, but . . .
he's also not really my type."

I think back to the story you told Joanna and me
about going on a college visit in high school
and hooking up with the captain of the lacrosse team
in a locker room.

But George Dale is shorter than you.
You're into the big, tall, strong lax bros.
Not the George Dale lax bros.

And now I'm rolling my eyes.
And I'm laughing.
And I couldn't care less about

stupid

freshman

George Dale.

BOY TALK

It's December, the semester is almost over,
and I'm studying your face,
wondering whether you feel sad.

I've yet to see you legitimately sad,
so I don't really know what to look for.

We're sitting across from each other
in the private study lounge
down the hall from my room.

Your expression remains fairly neutral as you
vent to me about Chris—
who was so big and muscular,
the hottest guy you will ever be with.

You sigh. And I ask whether you've been
watching the rest of the new *Real World*.

You tell me Chris got in a fight
with some random guy
at a club on the last episode,
as casually as you tell me that
he practically cheated on you
in front of your face.

For a moment, I imagine you sitting alone
in your room back in the German House,
smoking pot and watching clips
of your ex-boyfriend partying,

and I feel a deep pang
of sadness for you.

I've heard a few details
of your coming-out story,
but I've never talked
directly about it with you.

You tell me how you grew up
in a very Catholic household
outside of Boston. You wrote
in a prayer journal every day
in elementary school, and you
went to an all-boys Catholic high school.

You dated girls.

At the end of your senior year,
you gave a speech at a graduation event
and came out to all of the people who
watched you grow up as someone else,

much to the chagrin
of your high school girlfriends
and your very Catholic parents.

When you're finished telling me all this,
you turn to look out the window, and
my eyes fall back to the open books
and loose papers on the table between us.

I stare at the same page of
Tess of the d'Urbervilles

for the next ten minutes,
imagining what you went through
and hoping with all my heart
that one day you'll end up
with someone who will make you happy—

someone you deserve.

FINALS WEEK

Everyone's still cramming for finals,
but you and I have the rest of the week to waste.

We take some Molly in my room, just the two of us,
then dance on top of tables at a swim team party.

Soon we're rolling especially hard,
and we seek refuge in the stairwell.

The thunderous bassline of an A-Trak remix
of "Heads Will Roll" by the Yeah Yeah Yeahs
bumps over shouts and laughter.

Empty beer cans are littered everywhere.
A sticky layer of spilled drinks covers the linoleum.
But you and I could care less,
sitting on the stairs together,
unable to stop laughing.

I'm in a tight red dress with a green ribbon tied under my chest.
You're in a pink and green neon jacket and Santa hat.
I'm straddling your lap, admiring your eyes,
maniacally rubbing the stubble on your cheeks.

I laugh at a beer can that rolls down the stairs,
and then you lean into me and say,

"I think you're so beautiful. Did you know that?
I'll never stop giving you shit for being a dumbass,
but you are honestly so attractive
and such a fucking cool person."

My heart, already on steroids from the Molly, flutters.
I grab the Santa hat off your head and pull it onto my own.

"Well," I begin, "I'll admit you are seriously
the funniest person I have ever met. And you
have fucking beautiful, mesmerizing eyes."

You stare back at me with such intensity,
widening your eyes and tilting your head
like an animal, and we can't stop cackling.

I haven't felt this happy since
I was a little kid,
when all the scary stuff
was just pretend.

And now,
winning praise from you
gives me a reason
to start liking myself again.

OVER CHRISTMAS BREAK

My family always spends the holidays
at my grandparents' house near Boston,
coincidentally, just one town over from
where you grew up.

"You must be Susie Q!" you bellow
as you walk through the door
and give my mom a much bigger, warmer hug
than you give me.

I roll my eyes as you chat like old pals.

Then as we walk down the driveway,
you turn to me with a big smile on your face.
"No offense, Dalton, but it really makes
no sense that you're her daughter.
She is so warm and pleasant."

I shove you, and we get in the car, and you laugh,
"I felt like Straight Max from high school
meeting a girl's parents for the first time."

We drive through the winding streets
of my grandparents' neighborhood.
Christmas lights twinkle on the fences
and bushes of almost every front yard.

When we walk into your house,
your family is shouting emphatically
about the episode of *The West Wing*
flashing across the plasma, and

they debate whether I look more like
Claire Danes or one of your sister's friends.

Then I'm sitting on your bed
giggling at photos in your yearbooks.
This reminds you to dig through
the bottom drawer of your desk.
You pull out a notebook, and
I fall back in gasps.

Written in Wite-Out across the black cover
are the words "Christian Journal"
and your name underneath.

I can hardly contain myself as I flip through the pages.
"Your handwriting is so girly! This is not real."

"Oh, but it is."

Like every kid who's ever written in a journal,
Little Max is
bored, silly, and purely honest—
only, instead of "Dear Diary"
your entries begin with "Dear God."

And even though I'm laughing uncontrollably
as I read, there is no doubt that my
admiration and compassion
for you are swelling with each flipped page.

When I come to the entry dated 9/11/01,
my giggles subside, and

I look up from the journal at you,
sitting in your desk chair,
and I see you as a fourth grader:

Little Max doesn't understand exactly why
he has to write to a god who can never
know his true feelings,
or why those planes crashed into those buildings,
but he's trying to do what he's told is right.

I stare at you for a moment as a transitive sort
of sadness for Little Max sinks in.

When I was a kid, I hated going to church.
I hated wearing uncomfortable, ugly dress pants.
I hated sitting in the dusty, drab, windowless classrooms
watching weird preachy episodes of *VeggieTales*.

But most of all,
I hated the disturbing Bible stories we had to read
about children being sacrificed,
and babies being cut in half,
and people being forced into furnaces.

As we come to understand that Santa Claus
doesn't eat the cookies we leave out for him
and that leprechauns don't hide their gold
at the ends of rainbows, we're also told
that there used to be humans who
could bend water and rise from the dead.

Later, Pete comes over, and we sit in a circle
of folding lawn chairs in the shed,
and you and Pete recount detailed stories
of rebelling against your strict Catholic school rules.

And then we laugh all over again
about the traumas of adolescence
because laughing is all we have left
to make sad memories
worth remembering.

At the end of the night, when you drive me
back to my grandparents' house,
I feel bubbly and warm
and very pleasantly surprised
with how seamlessly we mix into each other's lives
outside of school.

I smile to myself as I walk up the front steps,
grateful for my closeness with you—like we've
been friends for years instead of months.

REFLECTIONS: I'M A LITTLE KID WHO LOVES

sparkly rocks in the stream
and smashing them to pieces
with the hammer from Dad's workbench.

My American Girl doll, Josefina Montoya.
Playing dress-up and house with Cate from next door.
Climbing trees and building forts in the woods.

LEGOs, and Game Boy, and Nintendo 64.
Hand-me-downs from my sister, Laura.
Hand-me-downs from my brother, Andrew.

Singing Celine Dion songs as loud as I can.
Making up knock-knock jokes in the sandbox.
Barbies, sports, and lots of attention.

MAX AND EMILY WORLD

We're back on campus in January.
When it's just us, we like to go to Ross Dining Hall.

"It's dead in here," you say as you walk
toward the stacked plates.

I sit down at an empty, gray particle-board table
and sip coffee from a white porcelain mug.

The high ceiling is patterned with glares
of late afternoon sunlight that reflect
off the veneered hardwood floors.
Dishware and silverware clink softly,
and the few other people in the massive hall
make it feel especially cavernous.

Three girls with tennis rackets share a plate of French fries
at a round table near the big west-facing windows;
an older man who looks like a professor cuts into a grapefruit
at a long table by the ice cream station;
and a gangly upperclassman wearing a coconut husk hat
stares intently into his laptop over near the doors.

"What'd you get?" I ask as you sit down
across from me with two red plastic bowls.

"Black bean burger."

We sit in silence for a minute or so,
you biting into your black bean burger
and reading an abandoned copy

of the *Middlebury Campus*
while I finish my coffee.

"What?" you ask through a mouthful.

I'm studying you cutting off little bites
of the patty in one bowl and then
dipping them in ketchup in the other bowl.
A smirk climbs up my face.

There's a dab of ketchup
in your dark blond beard.

We are both stoned
and probably reek of pot.

I sing the words
to the tune of "Blackbird" by the Beatles:

"Black bean burger . . ."

You take a sip from one of your two glasses of milk—
you always fill at least two glasses of 2% milk—
and finish the lyric:

"Black bean burger in the dead of Ross!"

I coo back, "Take these broken beans and make a burger . . ."

We sing alternating lyrics
of our stoned rendition of the classic tune,
laughing in spurts through the rest of the meal,
completely oblivious to our fellow diners.

Perhaps they're annoyed,
or bewildered,
or amused.

But none of it touches us
in Max and Emily World.

REFLECTIONS: FIRST KISS

Eighth grade.
Halloween.
It's a truth or dare—
Whitney tells Greg
and Greg tells Drew
and then we all go trick-or-treating.

(All my other girl friends
have already kissed boys.)

My heart is pounding
and my hands are shaking
as Drew walks me through the night
behind an evergreen tree
in the side yard of a house
on Fox Den Road.

I'm Raggedy Ann.
Drew's a soccer player.

He turns to face me.
Is it too dark
to see each other's lips?

The next thing I know,
we're hand in sweaty hand,
walking back to our friends in the street.

The following day, I have to ask Whitney
whether she's sure
I had my first kiss.

Her funny look confirms it.

But . . .

where did the memory go?

For the next week and a half,
I'm trying to put the pieces
of my first kiss
back together.

But all I have
are leftover scraps of cloth,
button eyes,
and some old red yarn.

If I can't remember,
does it still count?

THE ENTERTAINMENT

We're waiting in the common room for Luke—
a teammate of yours on the swim team,
a senior. We're waiting to buy pot,
but he's not back from his night class.
He tells us to hang here.

A soft buzz from the fluorescent ceiling lights
hums over the bumping of a bass on the floor above us.

"I'm bored. Entertain me," you say,
shaking the big messy bun
of blonde tangles on my head.

"How?" I say, uninterested,
not looking up from my phone
as I casually readjust my hair.

"I don't know. Let's make out."

I glance up at you and snicker.

"Come on," you sneer,
"don't be a prude.
Make out with me."

You lean over and grab my phone out of my hands.
"I haven't kissed anyone in a while," you say,
"I need to make sure I'm still good."

"Were you ever?" I tease.

You give me a look that
challenges my entire existence,
then pull me by my arm
on top of you
as you lie back on the futon.

I awkwardly half-resist,
then look down to find
that our faces are now
uncomfortably close.

You raise an eyebrow; I roll my eyes.
But before I have another second to protest,
you close the gap between our mouths,
and I mechanically follow your tongue's lead,
trying not to let my arms wrap
instinctively around you.

It feels like what I would imagine
an actor experiences
during a kissing scene:
not so much skill required
to act out the movements
as to stay in character.

We kiss for no more than thirty seconds
before the door opens, then slams in the foyer.
I jump away from you, and you sit back up,
smirking triumphantly.

Luke appears from around the corner
and starts complaining about his class.

I glance over to you. You're still
eyeing me deviously.

"Fuck you," I mouth to you.

We make our purchase and
say goodbye to Luke,
and I start down the steps
still wholly unsure
whether I feel angry and violated,
annoyed and used,
or flattered and withholding.

You lightly but intentionally jostle me
as you go by, two-stepping down the stairs,
and as you hop off the bottom step,
you shout back to me over your shoulder,

"You didn't exactly stop me!"

. . . And I guess you're right.

LATER THAT NIGHT

We just finished watching the finale
of *The Real World* on my laptop, and
we're lying side by side on my bed.

I follow your gaze to the cluster
of glow-in-the-dark stars stuck
on the ceiling overhead.

The weak hue of mint green struggles
to gleam through the dim.
Your eyes are trained like
you're waiting for one of them to fall.

When you turn back down to me,
I detect the tortured shadow of pain
in your eyes.

You tilt your head back up to the ceiling,
let out a heavy sigh, and force a brief smile.

You ask me, "Do you think I turned you
into a weed monster?"

I hesitate, unsure how to answer the question.

"Emily." You look alarmed now,
like there's something urgent
you need to tell me but you don't know how.

You take my wrist,
place my hand on your pants.

I let out a nervous laugh,
and we speak with our eyes:

What is going on? What is happening?

"I'm not really sure what's
happening right now, Emily.
But I think . . . I don't know.
I kind of liked making out earlier.
That might be it."

I try to allow my brain to process this,
projecting backward and forward
through our friendship as you continue.

"It was just . . . like . . .
really weirdly good.
Can we try it again?"

You ask me this as calmly and casually
as one good friend asks another for a simple favor,
no hints of pleading or pressure in your voice.

I feel oddly at ease.

You move your face closer to mine.
Pause.
This time, you look into my eyes to confirm,
and I meet you partway.

We kiss like we did in Luke's suite.
But this time, I move my body willingly
on top of yours when you pull for it.

The world around us stops,
or disappears,
or never existed
to begin with
while our bodies
find each other.

Our lips and tongues move
with the same magnetic friction
of our personalities—
both sides working feverishly
to challenge and dominate the other.

You slip your hands under my shirt.
Around my lower back.
You grind my hips down against you
as I bite your lower lip.

The heavy heat bursts like flames
through my mind, burning away any inhibition,
leaving only carnal impulse.

I let out a deep sigh as you rock
my waist back and forth, and you moan
into my ear, moving me harder and faster.

We're fully clothed,
in sweatpants and T-shirts,
horizontal on my twin bed,
tongues pressing against each other,
when the friction between us
pushes

me

over

the
climactic edge.

I attempt
to muffle
the sounds
and breaths

heaving

out of my

body

as you tighten

your arms around my torso,
hold my head against your chest.

You lie still
and stroke my hair
as I gasp for air on top of you
and settle in the afterglow.

Without moving
or looking up at you,
I inhale deeply, whispering a quiet
"What . . ." on the exhale.

You pull the covers up over us,
and I shift down next to you,
curled under your arm.

"I'm confused, Max."

"I am, too," you say.
"I feel like
I don't want to go
get in Joanna's bed right now.
Like, I don't want to stop
holding you."

THE MORNING AFTER

When I wake up, it's like the moment
I woke up after my tonsillectomy:
at first remembering nothing,
then everything,
then trying to assess the damage.

I remain very still in my bed,
huddled up against the wall.

Was that real? Was it all a strange dream?
When I turn over, will he be next to me?

I slowly roll onto my other side
and feel a confusing combination of joy
and disappointment
when I see you sleeping peacefully in Joanna's bed.

Part of me hopes
that what happened
last night
might
go unacknowledged for a while.

The only light in the room
comes through the cracks
in the drawn blinds.

I quietly gather my clothes and books
in the almost darkness,
trying not to wake you.

Just as I'm zipping up my backpack,
you speak. "Will you bring me noms
from the dining hall when you come back,
sweet duchess?"

I roll my eyes but smile,
relieved
that you're acting relatively normal.

Good, I think, *this might not change
anything between us, after all.*

REFLECTIONS: TWELFTH GRADE

It's a few days before Christmas
in my senior year of high school.
My family is gathered in our living room
watching the home video labeled:

CHRISTMAS 1991

My mom is eight months pregnant.
With me.

She turns toward the camera,
hand on her big round belly,
with a big round smile, and says:

"Our little Christmas surprise."

I snatch up the remote,
pause the TV, and whip around
to look at my mom.

I've always known I was a mistake.
But my parents have always denied it,
until they can't,
as the video plays before our eyes.

I rewind, shushing my parents and siblings,
then replay the scene.
My mom grasps at an alternative explanation—

"I just meant . . . Christmas *present*!"

but even she knows they've been caught.
And it's easier to laugh along
than to demand answers.

My eyes glaze over as the video cuts
to Andrew and Laura in a Christmas pageant.
I'm planning to ask more questions tomorrow
even though I think I already know the answers.
The true story is:

When my mom told my dad
she was pregnant
with number three,
his face went pale.
The plan was tuition for two.

On the TV screen, five-year-old Andrew
stands next to four-year-old Laura—
two little ginger kids singing "Joy to the World"—
but my brain is elsewhere, calculating
the total tuition of four years at Middlebury College.

I haven't gotten the official letter yet,
but a few days ago, the track coach emailed
to say that he hopes I'll be getting some
Midd apparel for Christmas
because I'm going to need it.

Later, after my dad and my siblings
have gone to bed,
my mom falls asleep on the couch next to me,
while reruns of *Seinfeld* play on the TV.

An episode ends.
The slap bass theme wakes her up.
And on her way to the stairs,
as she kisses my head,
she whispers softly to me:

"Some of the most beautiful
things in life come
from mistakes."

THE FIRST WEEKEND OF FEBRUARY

You get kicked out of the German House
for smoking too much pot and
move into Theo's suite in Milliken,
three floors above me.

We're sitting on your new bed, and I'm
telling you about how I saw George Dale
out at the Mill with his new girlfriend—

"Are you wearing a bra?" you interrupt.

I look down at the black cotton top hanging
from thin straps over my shoulders,
forgetting that some things that used to be
casual between us might not be
quite so casual anymore.

"You have nice boobs, Em.
They're small, but they're nice."

I grab my chest, "Well, you're right.
They are nice."

"And nice lips, too."
You lean in close to me,
eyeing my mouth.

I force your eyes up to lock with mine.
No boy has ever looked at me the way
you're looking at me right now.

The simmering desire on your face makes me feel
like some kind of all-powerful femme fatale,
daring you to resist me.

I'm feeling
exalted, confused, nervous,
all at once.

Your gaze drops down again to my lips,
and then you close your eyes, sighing,
"Emily . . ."

Your eyes
are open once again,
and you're
lunging
toward me.

Your tongue finds its way into my mouth,
and your hands squeeze my sides.
You push us down on the bed and
reposition yourself astride me.

Kissing you tastes so good,
which doesn't make any sense,
and I'm thinking that maybe there truly
is something chemical between us.

I read once about the science of kissing—
how the body can detect freakishly
specific data about your genetic

compatibility with someone
just by kissing them.

I press my palm to your chest and push back.

"You don't want to?" you ask.
"Or we can't? Because I think we can."

The truth is I do want to.

You start to kiss my neck.
I release the tension in my arm
that holds you back and allow it,
but only for a moment.

"Max, what is going on right now?"

"This," you say into my neck as you
angle your hips down against mine.

I gasp unintentionally.

You're taking this
as a signal to go further,
pulling down my shirt,
moving your mouth to my chest.

"We need to lock the door," I whisper,
because I know I'm toast.

My head rolls back into the pillow,
and my hips thrust up, trembling.

I can see the spark of fascination
in your eyes at this new discovery—
this new way to have complete control over me.

Then you move back up to my mouth
as your hand moves down under my skirt.
"Can I?"

You breathe heavily into my ear with an
urgency I can't deny, and as soon as I nod,
you nearly
rip my underwear off.

We're staring at each other
in awe.

This makes no sense
and total sense
all at the same time.

I knew you'd had girlfriends
in high school, but I did not know
you knew this much.

Everything is perfect—
every movement,
every amount of pressure,
every kiss,
every variation
makes it seem like every guy before you
was actually
clueless.

AFTER IT HAPPENS

I'm lying next to you
in your twin bed,
trying to catch my breath.

My gaze falls on the *Human Centipede* poster
tacked to your wall, and even though
there is nothing less sexy or more
disgusting than that movie,
I'm smiling and cuddling in closer to you,
because it reminds me of the first time
I watched it with you, how your
continuous guffawing made it impossible
to feel as disturbed and frightened
as I should've felt.

I'm smiling and cuddling in closer to you,
because you've taught me that it's okay
to take things less seriously
and sometimes, even, to laugh
at how absurdly scary life can be.

I'm not going to freak out about
what just happened between us.
I suppose it was just the fleeting product
of reckless, misguided impulse—
two meddlesome rebellion junkies,
bored of their current prospects on campus,
who just happen to have cooperative body parts.

It's not like having sex with you
will ever actually amount to
anything more than harmless experimentation.

Heck, maybe
        we'll do it again
if we can get through it
without laughing. . .
But then I'm sure
        we'll just end
up joking about how weird we're being,
maybe give each other shit for it,
smoke a few joints and
        move on.

THE SECOND WEEKEND OF FEBRUARY

We haven't exactly concluded
our harmless experimentation.

It's well past midnight when I emerge
from your room, missing a few articles of clothing,
to half a dozen pairs of eyes staring back at me.

Theo raises his beer. A smirk creeps over his face.
Douglas and Rob play beer pong on the coffee table
while Sophie and Ramona drink beer on the couch.

Our friends are not used to finding your door locked.

"We've been waiting to rip the bong for an hour!"
Douglas drops his Ping-Pong ball into a cup
and moves past me to join you in your room.

Rob gives me a strange look. "Sorry . . ." I begin.
Then his face softens into a warm smile.
"That's okay, Dalton. We weren't really waiting for an hour."
He gives my shoulder a nudge as he passes by.

A week later, you and I arrive back at your suite
in a drunken fit, and we don't even make it to your room
before your hands are all over me
and my clothes are coming off.

You push me into the bathroom and
lift me up on top of the recycling bin.

We're making out under the bright
fluorescent lights, entirely consumed,
until you start to unzip my pants.

"Max!" I have a momentary shock of worry.

"What?" You barely pause to let me speak.
"The door. Lock the door!"

It's a communal bathroom with two stalls,
and it isn't long before
we hear the door handle shake.

"Hello?" It's Theo's voice.

There's a knocking, and then
the handle shakes again.

"Is someone in there? Kind of need to get in . . ."

We muffle our voices as you throw clothing at me
and I hop down from the recycling bin.

"Max? That you?"

"Yep, one second."

"Sorry, dude. Need my toothbrush."

You make a casual excuse about
accidentally locking the door, and
I avoid eye contact with Theo as we scurry out.

Somehow, we're able to get away
with these kinds of escapades.

CLOUDS OF GRAY

When the snow has melted down
from the peaks of the Green Mountains,
filling the creeks
and softening the earth underfoot,
you and I have slept together

more than a dozen times.

The days grow longer.
Tiny buds sprout from branches.
Frigid water gushes under the bridges in town,
and our friends finally start to question
our bizarre behavior.

But my pragmatic attempts
to curb our romance,
restore our friendship,
only heighten your desire.

I tell you, "You need to hook up with guys,
and I need to hook up with guys."
You groan at the cloudy gray sky
darkening into night.

"It's confusing us both, Max.
You're my best friend."

You counter, "I don't know why
that means we need to stop
exploring this

                                                    bizarre,

beautiful

                    thing."

"Just all of a sudden
you wanted to have
sex with me?" I ask.

You think for a moment,
"Well, not really . . .
I remember watching you get dressed
after you showered one night
and then having this weird feeling
like I was seeing something

I shouldn't be allowed to see . . ."

CURIOUSER

I'm worried
that what's happening
between

     us

is like Alice's reaction to the

    White Rabbit.

Suddenly   realizing the anomaly
    of its   waistcoat pocket
      and   its watch,
    and then,   burning with curiosity,
  running across   the field,
  and going down   the hole after it,
never once considering   how in the world
            she's
            ever
           going
           to get
           out again.

ROB

Rob smiles and swings his keys around his fingers.
"Ready?"
"Just us?" I ask as we leave the library.

We talk and laugh in his brand-new Volvo,
all the way into town, and when we get to McDonald's,
Rob pays for my food without hesitation.

It's one of the first times Rob and I
have ever hung out alone—
without you—
and I'm not sure exactly what's happening.

I eat my cheeseburger and try not to overanalyze it.
But I notice the glimmer of a familiar feeling.

I guess I forgot what this feels like—
to hold the attention of a cute straight guy,
to flirt, to wonder, and to make him wonder
whether the interaction might go somewhere.

Could it possibly go anywhere?
Rob is one of the few people who
knows that you and I have hooked up.

He has the kind of eyes, hair, and body
that draw the attention of the most
popular, attractive girls on campus.
Why would he ever want to get with me—
the weird grungy stoner chick
who makes out with gay guys?

After our McDonald's date,
Rob keeps inviting me on late-night
post-library food runs in his fancy Volvo,
and it's hard for me to *not*
bashfully imagine a future with him.

And when I imagine that future,
I imagine a strong masculine figure—
someone who will always take care of me
and maybe even fawn over me.

One night, as we're walking back
from the parking lot to his dorm,
I stop and turn to him, ready to ask
if I'm not just imagining something
more than friendship happening between us.
But the look on his face answers my question,
and without thinking, I reach up to him,
and go in for the kiss.

When he picks me up
with his big, strong arms
so I can wrap my legs
around his torso,
I know this is going to keep happening,
and it pains me to imagine you
hearing about it from someone else.

A WEEK LATER

I break the silence between us to tell you myself.
And now you're pulling the hood
of your sweatshirt down over your face
and doubling over onto your knees.

We sit in silence for a minute.

"I've never been attracted to someone
like I am to you," you tell me.

"But don't you still want to be with guys?
I mean, you're gay."

The hopelessness on your face
softens into disappointment—
I should know better; I should know *you* better.

"I wish you could just see me as me
and not try to label me with stupid words."

I want to tell you that there has never been
and there will never be
any word
in any language
worthy
of labeling you—

worthy of saying
how I see you.

ZANDER

A week has passed since I told you about Rob.

I walk into your suite on the sixth floor
to find Theo and Ramona standing in the common room.
Ramona is wrapped in a towel,
and Theo is drinking a can of High Life.

"Is Max here? I think I left my bag in his room."

"He's in there. With Zander," Ramona says
in her signature monotone and points to the bathroom door.

The only Zander I know
is a gay guy
on the swim team
who you've been with
once or twice before—
the one who we laughed about
and imitated in robot voices.

I stare at the bathroom door
and hear the shower running.
I hear banging on the shower walls
and squeaking against the linoleum.

Ramona nods, and Theo chuckles.

I can't help but notice the unfamiliar pair
of sneakers on the floor next to your boots.
Then, the unfamiliar leather jacket hanging
over your desk chair.

Part of me feels terrified of actually seeing you
with this other guy, but then
a sense of peace, even happiness,
washes over.

You're hooking up with guys again!
We can just be friends, after all!
Maybe now everything can go back
to the way it was before.

Now I can talk freely with you about Rob,
and we can giggle about the details,
and you can tell me all about shower time with Zander,
and then we can compare notes on hetero and homo pleasure.

The shower is still running.
I sling my backpack over one shoulder,
wave goodbye to Theo and Ramona,
and leave the suite, smiling to myself.

BUT WHEN YOU AND I HANG OUT

it feels like a forced visit
between child and divorced parent.

And the more I feel
the strength of our bond deflating,
the less attracted I feel to Rob,
like losing you is his fault
in some sideways manner.

That he can't even come close
to making me feel the way that you do
only darkens the void.

When I'm with Rob now, some switch
inside my brain flips, and suddenly
I'm the girl I was in high school:
a girl who gave an admirable performance
but was not exactly herself.

This girl is committed to finding a strong, masculine husband
who will devote himself to taking care of her.
She's stuck thinking that she needs taking care of.

This girl hasn't yet considered it possible
that something different could
make her even happier . . . or
that she might be strong enough to take care of herself.

With Rob,
it seems,

I find myself
in character.

He's just so nice to me,
so easily pleased by how well I play the girlfriend.
It seems foolish to fantasize about something else—
about something more real.

A PREGAME IN ROB AND DOUGLAS'S DORM

The drink of choice is straight shots of cheap liquor.
I look around through the dim light, wondering
whether you've arrived yet.

An hour or so later Rob is shouting, "Let's go!"
and pulling me to the beer pong table.
I laugh as I take a Ping-Pong ball from his hand
and then look across the table
to measure up our opponents.

And there they are . . .

those icy blue eyes.
They stare straight into mine
from across the table.

They're all it takes to sober me up—
those eyes that see through my straightened hair
and dark mascara and still perceive beauty;
those eyes that can absorb all my pain
and reflect it back to me as something to feel proud of,
something that makes me strong and unique;
those eyes that have come to feel like home.

Next to you, Douglas is busy rearranging cups.
I watch your eyes as they move from me to Rob
and then back to me again.
The blue inside deepens
and then empties to a dull, distant glare.

For a split second, I wonder whether you
might just carry on and play.

You drop your neon orange
Ping-Pong ball into one of the cups.
You lean in to whisper a few words to Douglas,
then weakly pat his back and leave the table.
I watch you disappear into the hallway,
and, without another thought,
I tell Rob to find someone else to play with
and dash out after you.

The door to the far stairwell is closing.
I run down and swing it back open,
pulling with such desperate ferocity that
the handle leaves a dent in the adjacent wall.

You're halfway down the flight of stairs
when I shout after you.

You stop without turning and stand still
on the steps for a moment.
When you face me, your eyes pierce my heart,
and the expression on your face is unlike anything
I've seen before—a heart-wrenching mix
of agony and resignation—
and no trace of anger.

Your voice comes out soft and sad,
"Don't worry about it," as you turn back down the stairs.

I rush after you and grab your arm on the landing.
"Max, please, wait. I hate this. I don't want it to be like this."

Your head tilts as you breathe out
and look me straight in the eyes.
"You don't want it to be like what?"

I stare back at you, my heart pounding and my mind racing.
"Max, I miss you so goddamn much. I miss us.
And I don't know what to do."

The trace of anger that had been
absent from your face before
begins surfacing, welling in your eyes
and creasing the lines between them.

You're about to walk away from me as I hesitate in replying.

"I'm sorry, Max! I panicked, okay?
Everything got so confusing and weird
and scary between us, and I panicked!"

"You panicked so much that the only thing
you could possibly think to do
was start hooking up with my friend?
What did you even have to panic about?"

"About falling in love with you, Max!
About falling head over heels in love with you
and then losing it all—that's what!"

I choke up in shock and fear and regret
as I speak out loud this truth
I've been hiding, even from myself, for months.

The tension in your face slackens.
You take a step toward me.

I look into your eyes—
drains, slowly sucking me from reality,
out into an ocean of some sublime unknown.

"You're in love with me?"

"I don't know! Like, yes, Max!
I think I'm in love with you."

I wipe my eyes and turn away from you.
There's relief in finally saying the words,
but a tainted sense of it.

Even after all the kissing and cuddling,
after seeing each other naked
and touching each other's bodies,
I've been holding on to the hope
that we can return to being best friends.
Max and Emily World, right?

But saying those words—
admitting them to myself and to you—
puts it all in jeopardy.

You exhale, and your brow is furrowed again.
You lean back against the wall and look up
to the ceiling.

You close your eyes.

"Well, fuck, Em.
I'm in love with you, too."

IN YOUR EYES, I'M AS BIG AS THE SKY

It's a gorgeous spring day, full of sunshine
and warmth and budding new life.

We press the pieces of mushroom,
like seashell fragments,
into the peanut-buttered bread,
then blanket it with another slice.

It's Sophie, Theo, Paul, you, and me.
Each of us holding a small square of sandwich,
we cheers before biting into the day.

There's a subtle, acrid crunch.

I chew
and chew
and chew.

We wind through a field dotted with round bales of hay
wrapped in white plastic, like giant marshmallows
or globs of mozzarella cheese.

You climb on top of one,
sit with your legs dangling over the edge.

We come upon a stream with a narrow walking bridge.
Just a few planks of wood, barely wide enough
for two side-by-side bodies.

The five of us sit on the bridge, pulling apart cattails
and soaking our feet in the cool stream water.

Glimmers of sunlight dance around on the surface.

A pair of joggers approach,
and instead of following the four of you
to the other side of the bridge to make room,
I step down into the water,
and everyone laughs as my legs disappear into the stream
and my feet squish into the muck at the bottom.

Bright green reeds shoot up from the streambed
and sway around me,
calmly letting the current pull them
one way and the soft wind another.

Standing here next to the footbridge,
submerged in the stream from the waist down,
I realize, even after the runners have passed,
that I'm in no rush to get back out.

I'm doing something intuitive,
unexpected,
different from everyone else.

And I feel genuinely good
about doing my own thing, without an ounce
of concern about what anyone else thinks of me.

No fear of getting wet, of sinking my feet
into the unknown texture of the streambed,
of creepy-crawly creatures dwelling beneath the surface.

Today,
with the sun shining overhead

and reflecting off the ripples,
and the bright green stems
gracefully bending back and forth
against the current, the water feels
inviting and refreshing, and the mud at the bottom
oozes sensually between my toes.

I crane my head toward the sky and smile
at its unapologetic expanse.

And in this crystalline moment,
I love the endless blue for letting me feel
so inconsequential and small, like I can do and feel
whatever I want and it won't make any difference.

When I bring my attention back down to earth,
we lock eyes, and you smile at me
from the other side of the bridge.

And just like that,
I'm big again.

Big
but, somehow,
still free.

WHAT WOULD MICHELLE OBAMA DO?

It's Sunday morning,
and we wake up in your bed
still totally drunk,
and we're hung up
on how unfair it is that Michelle Obama
has to stay inside all the time.

She stares at me from the corner of your room—
a life-size cardboard cutout—
as we debate getting out of bed.
"What would Michelle Obama do?" I ask.

"She would go outside and organize
a Zumba class on Battell Beach," you declare.
"She so would," I reply flatly.

Twenty minutes later, we're walking
across the big open lawn that is Battell Beach,
holding Michelle between us.

We're quite the threesome—
Michelle in her formal turquoise pantsuit,
you in sweatpants and flip-flops,
and me in the tight dress from last night
under one of your soft flannels.

As we make our way to the dining hall,
students stop and stare.
Some of them shoot us judgmental glares,
some just laugh, and others,
the best of them, shout things like,

"Oh my god! It's the First Lady!" or
"Hi, Michelle! I love you!"

We allow photos and take them
for the random students
who want to pose with the First Lady
as we carry her through the breakfast line,
sit with her in the dining hall,
and lounge with her outside in Adirondack chairs.
Our friends text us about the celebrity spotting,
and a few of them come out to hang.

Anyone who doesn't know us would assume
we're conducting some kind of political
or social experiment for a class.
But those who do know us know the truth:

We're stirring up as much chaos
with as little effort as we can,
just for our own stupid entertainment,
here inside Max and Emily World.

LAST DAY OF SOPHOMORE YEAR

We're sitting on the stone wall behind Ross.

It's late and dark outside,
but I can see your face glowing
in the orange light of the burning end
of the spliff we pass back and forth.

I'm leaving tomorrow morning.
You're staying on campus a few more days.
And since I'll be in Prague and you'll be in Berlin
studying abroad next semester, neither of us knows
when we'll see each other next.

"Why does time have to happen like it does?"
I ask you, more as a rhetorical lament.

"Because we have lives to live
before we can really be together."

I turn to you, taken aback by such a statement.
"Really be together?"

"Yeah. Together forever."

I snort, but then I realize
there's no sarcasm in your voice.

"We would have the best wedding ever, wouldn't we?"

I smile, envisioning
the laughter,

the silly dance moves,
the beaming faces watching it all happen.

Your arm is around me,
and I can feel the warmth
of tears behind my eyes
as I move in closer to rest
my head on your chest.

Visions of boyfriends past
flash through my mind,
and I realize
how silly I was to have thought I'd known love
before this.

HEADING WEST

I take a job working at a dude ranch
for the summer with my sister, Laura.

We pack up Laura's car, Jane Honda,
and drive out to Creede in Mineral County, Colorado
near the headwaters of the Rio Grande.

Working on the 4UR Ranch—
an all-inclusive luxury resort-type of ranch—
is like summer camp for adults.

I'm on the housekeeping staff,
so each day, we're divided into teams of two
and make our way through the guest cabins,
one team to a room, until all the rooms are clean.

We ride from cabin to cabin
in golf carts filled with supplies.
We make the beds, vacuum,
clean the bathrooms, and restock.

Downtime on the ranch consists of
casting an aimless fly rod into the Rio;
competing to find the most antler sheds
during hikes through the mountains;
sucking the sweet nectar from Indian paintbrush wildflowers;
lounging on the back porch of a staff cabin,
soaking in the hot, dry sunshine,
listening to banjo music and
the echoing pops of BBs hitting beer cans.

I figure I'll be spending most of my free time
this summer on adventures with Laura,
or on the phone with you,
but then I meet Val.

VALERIE

She's one of my four bunkmates.
Her hair is jet-black.
She's got an unsettling tone of indifference in her voice.
She's distant and inaccessible in a way I don't quite understand.
Helpful words come out of her mouth,
but her tone and demeanor don't seem to match up.

She drinks often and a lot.
She always seems to be at the center of the party,
like a little dark-haired ringleader conducting the revelry
with a jug of Carlo Rossi hanging off one finger.

She's one of the best, most hardworking housekeepers.
She's always staying late in the laundry room
or offering to help out on the miscellaneous jobs
no one else wants to do.

She plays Adele and Avett Brothers songs out loud on her phone
and wears crop tops during work,
neither of which is allowed,
but she gets away with it because she works so hard.

Val loves little kids and refers to them as "boodles."
She has bizarre nicknames for almost all of the upper management,
like Paula, the breakfast chef, who she refers to as "DJ Paula D."
She often speaks in a squeaky, high-pitched voice
and uses made-up words to express her emotions,
like "ah-gew!" and "derpa derpa!"
and her laugh is as infectious as her dance moves.

While Val can be quiet and reserved at times,
her true self is silly, kind, and a little bit rambunctious.
She can make me laugh the same way Max can.

She refers to boobs as "Grand Tetons,"
and whenever she looks at herself in a mirror,
she'll always say, to no one in particular,
"Ooh, who dat babe?"

She loves to dance and becomes obsessed
with any song I play for her
that makes her want to put on her cowboy boots
and stomp around the bar in town.

A FRIEND WHO IS A GIRL

On an afternoon in late June,
Val and I get off work early
and take some beers down
to the pond and go fly-fishing.

The walk from our staff cabin
takes about fifteen minutes down
a winding dirt road and doesn't provide nearly
enough time to explain my love life
when she asks, but I try.

As I tell her about you,
fishing rod propped over my shoulder,
Val listens intently, warmly:
nodding, laughing, questioning, comforting
at all the right moments.

In the rowboat on the pond,
we crack open the PBRs,
and I tell her all about my
three boyfriends from high school—
how Franklin was nerdy but made me laugh
until my stomach hurt,
how Ryan was a rebellious guitar-playing
pothead who threatened to kill himself
when I broke up with him, and how
Simon was a popular pretty-boy jock with
an unusual affinity for mushy-gushy romance.

On the walk back, Val tells me
about the guys she's been with—

not many and nothing serious—and how
it's hard for her to trust people
because of her parents' messy divorce.

What I mistook at first
for indifference in Val
is actually gentle, patient compassion—
the kind that makes me feel hopeful
that I've just made a new lifelong friend.

We didn't catch any fish today, but
it was a perfect afternoon of fishing.

GIRLS ARE CONFUSING

Val shows affection through
innocuous physical contact—
a hand on the shoulder,
a soft pat on the back, that kind of thing.

And if she knows someone well enough,
she'll sometimes sneak-attack with a "salmon slap,"
a flat hand slapping between the thighs like a fish.

For most of the summer, Val's been having a thing
with one of the older fishing guides,
but after a night of drinking,
she'll often find her way into my bed
and snuggle into my side.

On certain occasions,
at a rowdy barn party,
or in the backseat on a ride
home from the bars in town,
Val will pull my face close to hers
and kiss me with tongue.

It's playful
and ends in hysterical laughter,
never escalating
like it did with us . . .

But sometimes I wonder
why she seems so aggressive,
almost as if she's mad at me.

BOYS ARE TERRIBLE

On a Saturday morning in late July
my eyes open, and my thoughts
stagger and crash into each other

> *where am i*
> *i don't know*
> > *what happened last night . . .*

> *why am i naked*
> > *why am i fully*
> *naked*

The underside of the bunk above me—
a faded blue mattress—sags
between crooked wooden slats;
the dark green polyester rug is littered
with a month's worth of clinging dirt and hay;
and a dreadful pile of inside-out clothes
is abandoned next to the bed.

I jerk my head to face the musty body lying
next to me under this gross, scratchy red blanket.

Through the dim morning light, I see
the ruddy complexion and the dark stubble,
and I begin to realize what I've done.

Henry is one of those guys on the staff
that all the girls know to stay away from.

He's a wrangler
who tried to flirt with Val
at the beginning of the summer.

I thought I hated him, so
how the hell did I get here?

I'm late for Saturday turnovers.
I've blacked out before but NEVER like this,
and as I frantically collect my clothes,
Henry rubs his eyes and tells me
he doesn't remember anything either.
I want to scream and throw things at him
until he does remember what happened—
until he gives me an explanation for why
I woke up naked in his bed—
but I have to get out of there
because I'm already so late for work.
I run back to my bunk, through the
backyards of the staff cabins, and
I think I'm going to throw up.

For the next few days,
I can barely bring myself to look at Henry
let alone demand more answers from him.

He might not have more answers.
And even if he does, then what?
I just take his word?

And now Val is buying me
a pregnancy test because
I messed up

my birth control pills
and Laura is sacrificing
a day off to drive me four hours to the nearest
Planned Parenthood for STD tests and

why

    am

    I

    so

        stupid?

MY HEART IS POUNDING

and my hands are shaking
with nerves as I dial your number.

It's ringing, and
an uncomfortable nostalgia
passes through me.

I wish I was calling
to tell you what happened
as my best friend
and nothing more,
but instead, I'm bracing myself
for disbelief, anger, and
accusations of betrayal.

When you answer,
I choke on air, realizing I've been
holding my breath
since I picked up the phone.

I explain everything about Henry
in short, panicked breaths.

After I've finished talking,
there's silence on your end.

It's broken by a deep exhale.

"God, Emily. That really sucks."

I hang my head and squeeze my eyes shut.
Before I can respond, you speak again.

"I wish I could be there with you."

And even when I admit to you that
I have no way of knowing whether I was
an unconscious drunk girl or
an insane, blacked-out drunk girl,
you comfort me and make me laugh.

"We've all seen Sexy Emily
trying to do her Sexy Face . . ."

I pause and take a deep breath,
unsure how to pivot from worries
of sleeping with Henry to worries
of sleeping with you.

"I was wondering whether you would
do me a huge favor . . .
and go get tested, too."

The moment I ask it,
I regret it—
turning this whole thing
around on you, who's done
nothing wrong, while I'm here,
being reckless, screwing up,
and basing irrational fear
on a stereotype.

But in your answer, your tone
is gentle and understanding in a way
that makes me deeply grateful
for how well you know me.

"I can definitely do that for you, Em.
I love you, okay?"

And my heart swells and hurts,
because I'm suddenly and intensely
missing you more
than I have all summer
and now

I'm falling in love with you
all over again,
as a best friend
and as everything else.

FOUR DAYS BEFORE I LEAVE FOR PRAGUE

On one of my last nights, Val and I splurge
on a bottle of champagne
and sit in the window frame
of the old barn hayloft,
drinking to negative test results
and a great summer.

"I can't believe you're leaving me this week,"
Val squeals, half hugging me.

I lean into her, and she tugs my ponytail.
Aside from my mother and sister, I've never felt
so comfortable being affectionate
with another female.

I take a swig and tug her ponytail in return.

She's staring back at me in a way
that makes me hasten to look away
and say something else.

"Are you going to take my bed when I'm gone?" I ask.

She takes a big pull and leans back.
"No. That's so depressing. But
Madeline said I could stay in her bed . . ."

She glances sidelong at me,
and for a quick moment,
I wonder
whether I'm supposed to feel jealous.

PRAGUE METRONOME

I'm in Prague
standing near the water in Old Town.
I look up and see it for the first time—

the giant Metronome up on the hill

—across the Vltava River,
an enormous red pendulum anchored to
a bionic steel-grated triangle, swinging lazily
from one side to the other and back again.

I cross the bridge and ascend the stone staircase,
which stretches down the hill like two massive arms
cradling a bushel of evergreens.

The Metronome sits on a gigantic concrete pedestal.
A huge skatepark extends all the way
to the trees hundreds of yards back.

Skaters swoop and grind,
their wheels echoing over the concrete pavilion.
Now I'm close enough to touch the timekeeper,
but its arm is no longer moving.

I sit on the cement wall directly under
the big bright red metronome,
dangling my feet over the edge.

I move back and forth through
my thoughts and memories,

searching for answers,
or at least the right questions.

I gaze out over the city with a visceral clarity,
as though I'm Emerson's transparent eyeball,
focusing in on one of the best shots it's ever captured.

The evening sky reflects the colors of hot coals on the river.
Arched baroque viaducts rise regally out of the water.
Gothic spires stretch heavenward,
puncturing the clouds like pokers in the embers.
And green pine branch silhouettes brush
the bottom corners of the horizon.

At the top of my periphery,
a power line hangs over the hill on which I sit,
slack with hundreds of tossed sneakers.

It's nice to imagine the lives
that were lived in each pair—
how each pair had once been new,
never worn or walked in,
and how many different steps
they had all taken before finally
coming to rest, tangled like bolas
around the power line in Letná Park.

I think I'm falling in love
with the contradictions
of this postmodern wasteland vantage
rising up over the skyline of Prague
on the crest of this big hill.

I look down at my feet and make a vow
to throw my ratty old black Converse sneakers
up with all the rest of the decaying footwear
hanging in effigy over the power line.

I love my ratty old Converse sneakers
more than any other pair of shoes I've ever owned.

They're ripping at the seams,
stained with red paint,
tattered, and smelly—
but they're still wearable,
and they still fit me perfectly,
so I can't bring myself
to get rid of them.

Until I first looked up and saw
the line of tossed shoes at the Metronome,
I had intended to keep them forever.

FROM PRAGUE TO BERLIN

It's only five hours by bus to visit you.
I lean my head against the window and admire
the horizon, glowing bright pink with sunset.

Just a few hours later,
my heart is racing, and I can barely keep
the dopey smile off my face as I step off
the bus and scan the empty lot.

We spot each other under
the fluorescent street lamps
and both quicken our paces.

I'm pleasantly surprised when
you immediately go in for the kiss.

On the U-Bahn back to your apartment
we cuddle into each other, talking and laughing, and
this is the first time since arriving
in Europe two weeks ago
that I truly feel at ease.

The next day, I'm standing in front
of Fernsehturm Berlin—the tall, skinny TV Tower
constructed in 1960s communist Germany
as one big middle finger to the cathedral-dominated skyline.

Legend has it, when the sun hits the dome
at the top of the *Telespargel*
(TV-asparagus, as it is comically called),

the light creates the shape of a cross,
otherwise known as "the Pope's Revenge."

I do the classic

Let me stand here and do this
so it looks like I'm touching the tip!

while you and your roommates,
Olivia and Charlotte, laugh
at how off I am with my aim.

Then we get on a boat that takes us
down the Spree River.

The tour is in German, so you whisper
brief translations to me
as we sail through the city
holding hands, newly in love
and newly in Europe.

AT NIGHT

We take some Molly
and spend most of the evening
getting lost on trains, ending up
at the food stands lining the bridge above Alexanderplatz.

Olivia and Charlotte devour döner kebabs
while we buy lollipops from a Rasta man
who's laughing at our massive pupils.

As we leave the food stands and walk
along the overpass, you and I fall behind
the girls and into our giggle world—
extra giggly tonight.

It's a wasted night,
a wasted tax on our melting brains,
and a waste of a lot of train-ride fare,
but somehow you make the trash
feel like treasure.

As we get closer to your apartment,
just a few more blocks,
you make a casual comment
about spending the rest of our lives together.

This makes me smile.

"So we're not going to sleep
with other people then, right?"

The stutter in your step and the look on your face
throw me into slow motion, an unraveling
that fast-forwards and rewinds in all directions.

Your giant eyes gleam through the dark,
searching my face,
hoping, I can tell,
not to find it looking serious.

I titter nervously, still clinging to optimism
as you take my hand and keep us walking along.

You say, "I kind of figured we're
gonna be together forever, so
might as well be young and hot now,
while we still can."

young and hot while we still can

Before I've got time to process
your forward-thinking backward reasoning,
you whisk me away
into another conversation
and dance us all the way home.

The real world often feels
like it's crashing down on me
in one way or another.

But tonight, it's
my preciously remodeled version
of Max and Emily World

that has suddenly grown
painfully heavy.

The next time we see each other
will be in Munich at Oktoberfest in a few weeks.

And it sucks to wonder
whether we shouldn't have booked
that hotel room together
back in the middle of the summer.

REFLECTIONS: FIRST BOYFRIEND

Seventh grade just started.
Timmy and I have never actually
talked to each other in person.
But we talk on instant messenger
every day.

And sometimes,
we even talk for hours,
late into the night
when I should totally
be sleeping.
But I just can't
say "bye" to him.

After a month,
we put each other's initials
in our AIM profiles.
Then we go to the movies,
and he holds my hand the entire time.

Another month later,
he says he loves me.
And I say it back

over instant messenger.

HIGHLIGHTS OF OKTOBERFEST

Watching countless people stand atop
long biergarten tables and attempt
the full-stein chug.

Posing for an Italian photographer
who squirms around on the ground
for the perfect angles.

One of Joanna's friends from high school
falling asleep while standing in line.

An endless supply of rotisserie chicken platters.

You flirting in German with a middle-aged woman
who insists on reapplying her deep-red lipstick
before planting a kiss on your cheek.

Joanna peeing under one of the tables
in the tent because the bathrooms might
as well be mosh pits.

Hot German boys in lederhosen challenging
Joanna and me to drink beer from our shoes—
which we do, a worn leather boot tipped up
to Joanna's lips and one dirty old Converse up to mine.

Constant music, singing, and dancing.

And a shattering of language barriers
because everyone speaks the jubilantly unifying
language of beer.

LEAVING OKTOBERFEST

At the end of the weekend,
when it's time to depart the festival grounds,
you, Joanna, and I follow the dreary
mass exodus to the Munich bus station.

We pass by an American woman in her fifties or sixties
with a Midwestern accent and a mean scowl,
pumping a sign about Jesus into the air
and shouting about everyone's sins.

"He is all-powerful! He will punish you!
Jesus Christ our Lord, our one eternal Lord!
He will see that all sinners burn in hell!"

You can't resist.

You frolic over to the patch of cement
she occupies and start to yell
with her,
at her,
and over her,
much to her palpable distaste.

"God bless us! Everyone!" you shout.
"May peace be with you, and also with you,
and with you, too! My God is an awesome god!
He reigns from heaven above!
Jesus loves me! This I know! Don't you know?"

"Sinner! You're a sinner!" she barks at you.

"What if GOD was one of us?" you yodel.
"Just a SLOB like one of us?"

"All of you! SINNERS!" she shrieks.
Her gaze falls on Joanna and me, standing off to the side.
"You are NOT God's children!"

"Smite me, Lord! I'm sinning!" you shriek.

Then you toss your German flag scarf
around her back and lasso her into a dance.

She swats you away with her sign,
uninterested in dancing with a bibulous devil.

I wish I could laugh
or join in your counter-heckles,
but we have to leave each other soon,
and we're not just carefree friends
doing stupid shit anymore.

I grab you by the arm and drag you away,
the woman shouting after us, waving her sign in the air.

As we continue on toward the exit,
you spring about in front of us,
shouting "May the Lord be with you!"
to everyone we pass.

"What did you say?"
The guy is tall,
American, late-twenties, and has
a long dirty blond ponytail.

He approaches you with a sinister look.

"May the Lord be with you!"
you offer again enthusiastically.
But when you start to frolic away,
the guy grabs you by the shoulder.

"You have something to say to my friend?
Say it to my face." He gestures to his three friends,
but even they are backing off a little.

You sober up a bit, sensing danger.
"Dude, I was kidding. I wasn't talking to your friend."

Joanna and I watch nervously
as the guy interrogates you.

"Oh, I think you were talking to him.
Say it—say it to my face," he grunts.
"Come on, say it to my face, fairy!"

Now he's tightening his hold on your shoulder,
and something snaps inside of me.

I bolt forward. "He wasn't talking to you, dude—
so get the fuck away!"

I step in between you and push
ponytail boy away.

He attempts to curve around me, reaching for you,
and again, a protective instinct kicks in.

Without thinking, I push him again,
this time pressing the palm of my hand
against his face.

"Fuck OFF, dude!"

He stumbles back and looks up at me in disgust.
If I've ever tried to kill
with my feminine gaze,
it's right now.

"Oh yeah, let a GIRL fight for you, PUSSY!"
he yells after us as we hurry away.

I can't resist turning around
to get the last word.
I give him the finger.
"Go fix your PONYTAIL, honey!"

He's still shouting as we quicken
our pace to distance ourselves.

Then moments later, he's out of sight,
and the three of us burst into laughter,
recounting the look on his face when I
pressed my palm into it.

And even as you and I are about to part ways,
a jolt of adrenaline lifts my spirits.

On the bus back to Prague, I try to hold on
to the good parts of the weekend,

but my mind wanders skeptically
around that last interaction—with ponytail boy.

What a perfect opportunity it was for me
to play the woman card in my split-second reasoning—

I'm a woman, and he's a man.
I can get away with putting my hands on him,
and there is no way he will dare
to penetrate my gender shield.

But then, what if I had been a man?
What if I had been a gay man?
Trying to jump in and protect you . . .

And now I'm all confused,
asking myself whether I was using my gender
to show you what you can't get from a man,
or whether you were using my gender
to show men what they can't take from you.

As Joanna sleeps soundly in the seat next to me,
I stare blankly out the bus window,
thinking about everything
but seeing nothing
but white smoke
and the darkness of your sigh,
and the white smoke fades, and we're
on the hotel balcony last night,
and you're asking me how I'm
going to deal with you
still being attracted to guys.

"But that's what being in love is—" I say,
"not acting on the side attraction. Right?"

"I don't know, Em . . .
I think love
can be
a lot

of different things
for different people."

REFLECTIONS: SECOND BOYFRIEND

At the beginning of tenth grade,
my neighbor brings his friend Franklin
camping with our families on Labor Day weekend.

I've seen Franklin at school before;
he's in the grade above me.

Sitting around the campfire,
he makes a witty joke and plays
a really good song on his phone by a band
I've never heard of.
His glasses are kind of nerdy,
but I think he's cute.

A month later, we're dating,
and a few months after that,
we're so in love.

I think I'm going to marry him.

YOU VISIT ME IN PRAGUE

"But seriously. I need your body. How can I have it?"

I love hearing you say these words,
but I also hate how much I love it.

We stand in the shower kissing,
our bodies pressed together.

I hesitate before kneeling down—
something I've never done with you.

Up until now, you've always been the one doing things to me.

You stop me.

"Your soft, lady touch kind of just tickles."

I'm trying not to look upset
as I stand up,
tilt my head back under the water,
and smooth my hair away from my face.

THE DAY BEFORE YOU GO BACK TO BERLIN

The afternoon sky turns a bright gray
as we sit on a bench underneath
the Žižkov TV Tower.

I stare up the length of the three
chrome trunks of the tower—
originally built to intercept
anti-communist radio transmissions.

For years after the fall of communism,
it stood there like a misplaced toy rocket ship
dropped in the middle of a baroque diorama.

Then, in 2001, an artist named David Černý
was asked to improve its appearance.
He sculpted giant black fiberglass babies
and fixed them on the tower as if
they were crawling up and down it.

I've been looking forward to bringing you here,
to the Žižkov Tower,
because it's such a bizarre-looking structure
in this senseless shrug of city—
not to mention "diaper" is one of your favorite words.

I think you will find it
just as fascinatingly weird
as I do.

But when I point out the massive babies,
you merely snort and make

some disinterested remark
about how they look more
like ants than babies.

I'm noticing lately that
you're not gazing at me as often,
not cuddling into my side;
you're being a bit less hand-holdy,
which is fine; that happens.

. . . I googled it once back in high school
when I started to feel bored
with my third boyfriend, Ryan.

I clicked through article after article
looking for a logical explanation,
until—aha!

The honeymoon phase has to end
so that the couple can start focusing
on procreating and taking care of children . . .

Just a few days ago, when you arrived,
we made love in the shower, and then you
held me in my bottom bunk bed, whispering
cute jokes about our future children.

"They're all going to have red hair."

"Nooo," I groaned.

"Yes. We're going to lead a tribe
of little gingers with blue eyes.

You'll be a business-diaper
and bring home the bacon,
and I'll be the fun stay-at-home dad."

"Why do I have to be the business-diaper?"

You scoff, "Because you're not good with kids . . .

. . . and I'm not tough enough to be a business-diap."

And now I'm wondering whether you feel inadequate, too . . .

I know I can't always give you what you need—

but I also know how hard it was
for you to hide who you were
for so many years, then finally
feel open and proud . . .
and then fall in love with me

a girl

and how much harder that must make it
for you, straddling your shame-filled past
and our unpredictable love.

Beneath the tower, tension builds
as you scold me
for doing too many party drugs
with the "frat boys" in my abroad program
who live on the third floor.

I stare into the bare butt
of the lowest baby,
part of me envying the simplicity
of crawling around on all fours,
just innocently exploring the world,
and part of me trying to decide
how to react to what my gay
pseudoboyfriend has just implied.

You don't say it outright, but
you're suggesting that
if I do too many drugs,
my uterus won't be healthy enough
to bear your child.

I'm probably the only lover
you'll ever have
who can give you one of your own.

REFLECTIONS: SECOND BOYFRIEND, CONTINUED

It's late in the spring of tenth grade
and I'm practicing baton handoffs at track practice when
one of the older girls sees Franklin
waving to me from the parking lot.
I tell her that he's my boyfriend.
She looks confused and says:

"Oh, I always thought he was gay!"

I laugh, but I'm confused, because
sure, he's a little dorky, but he's obviously not gay.

The gay kids at our high school
are all friends with each other;
they're artsy, or emo,
and in the school plays.

In this mostly white upper-class suburb
in Connecticut, the kids who openly defy
the "good" stereotypes—Jock, Smart, Pretty—
are assigned the "bad" stereotypes:
Weird, Nerd, Gay.
United by their oddness.
Outsiders together.

I wave back to Franklin.

THE NIGHT BEFORE YOU GO BACK TO BERLIN

We walk through the gardens
and courtyards of *Pražský hrad*—
Prague Castle—at one in the morning.

The rain has stopped, and
the fog hangs thick and green
in the spotlights that
beam up the castle walls.

We sit next to each other
on the wide, damp steps
and stare out into the mist
falling over the Vltava River.

You're telling me that you think
you need to be with boys again.

You wait for me to say something.
I look up at you, tears threatening my eyes.

You continue, "I don't think I'm
going to be able to know what
I really want until I'm old.
Like, twenty-eight."

Twenty-eight.

I stare into your eyes,
wishing I had never met you,
angry at you, angry at myself
for believing I could

keep you
straight.

The next morning, I watch your bus
disappear around the corner,
and I continue to stand there,
staring off into empty space.

Seven years till twenty-eight . . .

a lot of empty space.

REFLECTIONS: THIRD BOYFRIEND

A week after I dump Franklin,
Ryan and I meet at a house party
in the middle of the summer before
junior year, and we're both wasted
on water bottle vodka and somehow
end up making out all night in the
parents' bedroom, and in the morning,
he's sweet and makes me laugh.

A month later, we're dating,
and a few months after that,
we're so in love.

I'm going to marry him.

PRAGUE METRONOME, CONTINUED

I visit the Metronome many times
throughout the semester, sometimes
with others but usually alone,
drawn to the sublime view—
to my own lack of understanding
for its origins and meaning.

A massive statue of Joseph Stalin once
stood on the pedestal atop the hill
where the Metronome stands now.

Though his dense granite head was blown off
shortly after its installment in 1955,
the Metronome didn't take his place
for another thirty years, in 1991,
after the Velvet Revolution triggered
the fall of communist regimes and Soviet control.

A metronome seems a fitting symbol for
the link between the Czech Republic's
newly established democracy
and its inescapable communist past.

The kinetic energy
meant to keep the seventy-five-foot arm
ticking back and forth often ebbs,
causing the arm to fall still
on one side or the other—
momentum stuck in place,
waiting to be wound up again.

The spot still conveys the notion of the place
where Stalin once stood over the city.
Yet the Metronome prevails over those
stale and shameful memories
with something he could never control:

time.

And as I sit here beneath the Metronome,
dangling my Converse over the edge,
breathing in this ancient city of spires
that labors to distance itself from the past,
my thoughts keep coming back to you—

how I'm in love with a boy
who needs more time before
he can be in love with me.

KAFKAESQUE

I wonder whether Kafka
might have been
secretly gay.

A hundred years ago,
Kafka met Felice Bauer,
and they had a tumultuous
five-year relationship,
constantly ending and picking
back up again.

He lived in Prague,
she lived in Berlin,
and all the while,
they hid their true selves
behind letters sent back and forth
across borders.

Well, mainly Kafka did.

He often canceled plans
to meet in person. He broke
their engagement to be married—twice—
and he was painfully cryptic
in his letters to Felice.

My professor is having us read
one of the letters out loud in class.

I start feeling anxious and sweaty,
and my heart is pounding, as if
a taunting spotlight is singling me out.

Paragraph by paragraph, the letter
makes its way through the rows.

With Kafka's words closing in on me,
my hands start to shake, and
I'm back on the Prague Castle steps
in the middle of the night.

I can hear the distant voice
of my classmate reading
but I'm watching your mouth move:

"... *I love you to the limits of my strength.*
But for the rest I do not know myself completely ..."

The rain falls faster, heavier.
The letter makes its way to my row.

"... *whether it is possible for me to take you*
as though nothing had happened,
I can only say that it is not possible ..."

I want to scream at you and push you
down the castle steps, but the rain
is flooding the river over the cobblestones.
The current is growing stronger against
our bodies, and I think I might drown.

There are two students between me and the letter.
The rain on our skin is hot.
Steam rises from the river around us.

". . . But what is possible, and in fact necessary,
is for me to take you with all that has happened,
and to hold on to you to the point of delirium."

I want to carve the number twenty-eight
into your flesh (you'd just laugh, anyway)
so you won't forget what you told me:
that you'll know what you really want
when you reach that age.

Instead, I kneel in front of you.
I tell you I'm sorry.

And now we're in the shower at Máchova,
and all of my classmates are watching
while I try unsuccessfully
to give you a blow job.

They're laughing at me.

LIKE FELICE

Felice saved all of Kafka's letters,
but most of her letters to him
are gone now.

I imagine how we'd sit at a bar in Old Town,
Felice and me, drinking cocktails.

"Why do we let these men toy with us like this, Felice?" I'd ask.

Felice would shake her head and sigh,
"Because we've never met anyone else like them."

"Cheers," I'd groan, and we'd clink glasses
before downing the last of our drinks.

BRUGES FOR THANKSGIVING

On our first day in Bruges,
cold rain comes down hard
in the morning but dissipates
into a foggy sprinkle by
the time we leave the Golden Tree.

The sidewalk is slick with a patina
of bright yellow wet leaves.

We take selfies with swans
on the edge of the canal.

We walk around the perimeter of the market square,
admiring the massive bell tower
and eating frites dipped in mayo.

We wander along a canal on the hilly outskirts
of town, past large windmills.

We take a boat ride through the city,
under low bridges, past medieval stone architecture.

We stroll through a garden
and hang out with more swans.

I take in the quaint history
of a romantic city
with the person I love.

OUR SECOND DAY IN BRUGES

We force down the truffles,
chase them with some Belgian chocolate,
and smoke two joints on the balcony,
the world slowly funneling into the confines
of the hotel room at the Golden Tree,
taking us along with it.

Soon there is no outside,
       no weather,
              no Bruges,
                     no Europe,
no planet Earth—
just us, willing prisoners.

We lie in bed for a while, staring
at the picture of the red flower
that hangs on the wall.

And then we're rolling around in sweatpants,
giggling and shrieking
in a composition
of joy and terror,
fascinated by
and terrified of
ourselves.

Somewhere in the deepest throes
of the trip, I cannot stop
cry-laughing and laugh-crying
into the pillows on the bed.
I've never experienced such

duality of emotion, like I exist only
inside the space between
opposing feelings.

I am happy and sad,
lost and found,
loved and left.

I am everything and nothing
that falling in love with you has made me feel.

Sometime around 10 p.m.,
we remember there is a world
outside that little red room.
We pull on coats and hats and boots
like we've never dressed ourselves before.

We walk out into the hall,
as if into a funhouse dream.
I try to remind myself that
there is nothing to be scared of.
We can't yet speak in full sentences.

We find an eerie bench
in an alcove
of an old church.

The massive brownstone is
alight in tiny spotlights that
catch the microscopic drops of water
falling through their beams.

The grass underfoot and the shrubbery in the courtyard
look synthetic green in such a dark corner of time and space.

You and I fit well into this film noir—
I can see it now . . .

Two lovers sit side by side in silence, passing a smoke back and
forth. They've just faced down their greatest fears—life, death,
art, love. They aren't sure they liked what they saw. They once
thought the love they shared had given them new life . . . but now it
could be the death of them. The fog thickens as they sink into the
shadow of their heavy bodies, blowing smoke up into the clouded
night sky.

Sitting on the bench near the church,
I return to my physical place in the real world—
and then succumb pathetically to an empty stupor.

We return to our hotel room and get back in bed,
lying on our sides, staring into each other's faces,
trying to channel our thoughts back into focus.

The overwhelming sensation of consciousness
still hasn't dulled, and restful sleep is like a final destination
that keeps moving farther and farther away.

You turn to lie flat on your back.
"What are you thinking?" I ask you.

"I don't know. I just can't keep staring
at you like that.
I feel weird and dead."

The next day—our last day in Bruges—
we pack up our things and leave the Golden Tree,
two heartsick zombies.

The weather has finally cleared,
and a bit of sunlight shines through
as we walk aimlessly down side streets,
past fountains, and over small footbridges.

The few words spoken between us are brusque and faltering.

I know the weekend has turned out to be a failure.
And I can sense that you're feeling
a growing resentment toward me for all of it—
like it was my fault the weather had been bad
and we had stayed inside too long
and we had felt so scared and confused.

The train ride back this Sunday afternoon
is so crowded with flocks of weekend travelers
that we can't sit near each other.

My mind and body feel so devoid
of their normal capacities to function
that I can't even figure out how to sleep.

I sit listening to songs I don't
even like that much anymore.
But I barely hear them anyway.

REFLECTIONS: FOURTH BOYFRIEND

Ryan got drunk and cheated on me,
so we aren't *really* together,
only *kind of* together still, when
I break it off completely and then
make out with his friend Simon
at a party on New Year's Eve.

Ryan has some kind of mental breakdown and
says he's going to kill himself,
and my mom
has to call the police, but
once that settles, Simon and I
start dating and fall so in love.

It's the worst that I have to break up with him
because he's going to UCONN
and I'm going to Middlebury,
because I'm, like, ninety percent sure

I'm going to marry him.

YOUR HEART'S IN MY SHOES

It's the end of the semester,
shortly after midnight in December.

I sit next to you on the frosty ledge
under the Metronome in Letná Park,
taking in one last bittersweet view of Prague.

I've fantasized about this moment
since the first day back in August
when the span of the Atlantic
felt so despondently infinite.

Tonight I've come prepared
with my old tattered Converse
tucked inside my purse.

I'm scanning the line of shoes
above us with a smile,
but as I look over at you,
I hate how deeply the sadness
of leaving you penetrates
my excitement to go home.

I'm realizing how different you look
from when I first met you.

Your face is much thinner,
and your dirty blond hair is longer.
You've started dressing differently, too.

Skintight pants and boots
in place of old khakis and sneakers.

"I miss you already, Max. It hurts."
I lean into you.

"I know, honey. It hurts everywhere."

I was hoping it wouldn't come up—
that maybe you should, for our sake,
explore your sexuality,

"do the gay thing"

these last two months
while you'll still be here in Europe
without me.

I close my eyes and breathe deeply.

We spend the rest of the night
sitting under the Metronome in limbo,
and it feels like you're an intruder
in my special place.

I invited you in, but
I didn't realize how much space
you would take up.

I have no one to blame but myself.

The next morning, going through security at the airport, I realize
that I forgot to toss

sneakers

Converse   up

old   over

ratty   the

my   line.

WHITNEY

Returning to campus for the start of winter term,
I can hardly crack a smile
at a group of freshmen sledding
down a hill on dining hall trays
or a herd of senior guys bombarding
each other with snowballs.

Everything around me
is a reminder of you,
and through messages and FaceTime
you can sense my depression.

You know you can't
be the support I need,
across the ocean in Europe,
so you recruit Whitney,
my best friend from home.

Despite being swamped with work
and busy with indoor track,
she comes for a quick weekend visit.

Whitney and I pregame with a bottle of Fireball
and blast some of our favorite high school anthems.

We pour one out to "Ghetto Gospel,"
the Tupac song Whit named my car after,
and we botch the dance moves she made up
to "Break Your Heart" by Taio Cruz
for an impromptu flash mob at our senior prom.

We make it out to a party but stay
only long enough to do "da stanky leg"
to a few songs before going back
to listen to our favorite Third Eye Blind jams.
And nothing new or exciting happens, but
I feel like I've been cleansed or reborn,
or something spiritual like that, because
I laugh more tonight than I have in months.

Three weeks later, when you finally
return to me, I jump
into your arms as soon
as they're free of luggage.

VALENTINE'S DAY

For weeks I've insisted
you STOP saying "I love you."

"Fine, I won't say I love you," you say.

"Thank you."

"I'll just come up with something else
that means the same thing—"

No rose petals.
No chocolates.
No teddy bears.
On Valentine's Day
you cover my bed
in diapers.

Diapers . . .

bursting from my drawers,
hanging in my closet,
tucked into my winter boots
and my track spikes
and my ratty old Converse sneakers.

Diapers strewn all over the floor.

One diaper, propped up against my pillow,
has a note in black marker:

My Diaper Only Sweats for You.
Happy Valentine's Day.

I laugh and I cry, and
my heart breaks apart into pieces,
melting.

You clear some of the diapers
from my bed and sit next to me.
You hold out a small blue pouch—Tiffany Blue.

I open it up and pull out
a tiny misshapen heart
hanging from a delicate silver chain.
You laugh and say,

"It's my deformed heart."

And I'm in disbelief—the good kind.

Then you make a joke about how
you never thought you'd be
buying jewelry for a girl
on Valentine's Day,
as you help me with the clasp.

And it's weird.
And it's perfect.

Now here we are surrounded by diapers,
and you're pouring cheap champagne
into red plastic cups on my desk.

You hand one to me and take
the other for yourself,
raising it up high.

You clear your throat theatrically and make a toast:

"To graduating from Pampers to Pull-Ups.
Babe, my babe, will you be my official babe?"

I roll my eyes
and heave a sigh,
but there's nothing sarcastic
about the way I kiss you.

YOU'RE FINALLY MY BOYFRIEND

and it lasts about a week.

INVITE ONLY

At the beginning of the week
I help you convert the twin bed frame
in your dorm room into a double
with a large sheet of thick plywood.

We slide Sophie's donated double mattress
up over the wood and then stretch
your gray cotton fitted sheet around the corners.

The bed now takes up three-quarters
of the tiny single dorm room,
but, "It's fine," you say,
because "all we need is this big bed
and each other."

And then you fall down onto the mattress,
and you pull me down with you into a long kiss.

At the end of the week, we lie in your bed,
side by side on our backs, and we stare up
at the ceiling and grumble back and forth
to each other about how many nights a week
we should be sleeping in the same bed.

"Three nights a week. And it should be
an invitation . . . not assumed."

You're telling me how sometimes
you just want to stretch out
like a starfish in your bed at night.

But all I'm hearing
is how
you don't sleep well
when you have to share your bed
with me.

We go to sleep
without saying goodnight,
and in the morning
I ask you whether we're in a fight.

You look like you're sorry,
and I already know why.

"Maybe
I'm still not ready
to be in a real relationship
with you."

I feel like an idiot for believing
we could finally work, but
it's easier to be mad at you
than at myself.

WINTER CARNIVAL

Last night, I made out with A.J. Peterson
behind an ice sculpture, and I guess
some people saw.

You and I sit across from each other
at the kitchen table in Palmer, tapping ash
into an old teacup and arguing about
our relationship while a rowdy, drunken snowball fight
carries on outside and "Call Me Maybe" blasts from the
basement.

You like to make up nicknames for all
my exes and flings, and when
you angrily refer to A.J. Peterson as
"Diap-Diap Diaperson,"
neither of us can keep a straight face.

And now we're laughing hysterically, starting
an ongoing joke about how all my exes have
a Facebook group together and
you and Diap-Diap Diaperson
are the newest members.

COURSE EVALUATIONS

I'm taking Modern Logic because
I need a math credit, and by the time
I'm done with the final exam, my brain
is at one percent battery life.

I'm staring down at the course evaluation form now,
the columns of empty circles lined up behind
bolded words—

Strongly disagree
Disagree
Neither agree nor disagree
Agree
Strongly agree

—my eyes start doing that thing
where the words blur out of focus
and then the world blurs out of focus
because I wish I could give you
an end-of-semester evaluation
to answer on the Likert scale:

I am gay.
I am straight.
I am bisexual.
I am jealous.
I am confused.
I am delusional.
I am in love.

SECOND SUMMER AT THE RANCH

It's not hard for Val to convince me
to return for another season at the 4UR Ranch—
this time, without my sister.

That's how I meet Grant.

He's a twenty-five-year-old ranch hand from Athens, Georgia,
who looks like a dad model in an L.L. Bean catalog,
but slightly sinister,
with his piercing blue eyes
and pointed canines.

Grant has a girlfriend back home,
and there's something about the way he smiles
at all of the female staff and teases them
that irks me.

So I avoid eye contact when I drive by him
in the housekeeping golf cart
and when he drives by me
on the riding lawn mower.

But I can't always avoid interactions
with him because one day I need to radio him
to bring a cot from storage to a guest room,
and the next day to set and check mousetraps in the lodge,
and a week after that to help a few frantic housekeepers,
caught in an afternoon downpour,
get the back wheels of their cart out of the mud.

And then, at a staff bonfire down near the Rio,
I'm sitting next to Val, drinking a Corona,
when Grant lunges in front of me and knocks
my beer bottle into the grass, sloshing foam
all over my T-shirt and jean shorts.

"What the fuck, dude?"

Before I can say anything else,
Val shrieks, and one of the waitstaff guys
down near the riverbank shouts out an "OH MY GOD"
that echoes against the ridge beyond the bonfire.

Grant stares into my eyes as he gets up
and dusts himself off, and it's now registering
that while he did just forcefully push me
and spill beer all over my clothes and his,
he also just jumped in front of me
to keep a speeding soccer ball
from hitting me
square in my face.

HARD TO GET

Now there are whispers that Grant
has broken up with his girlfriend, and
wet, hot steam tumbles out from the
stainless steel panels of the industrial dishwasher
as he walks into the Dish Pit kitchen
where I'm rinsing soup and salad dressing off
the first round of dinner plates.

At the end of our shift, Grant catches me
stealing a cookie from the guest cookie jar, and
my heart pounds in my chest as I mutter,

"Just making sure they're stocked."

And then he sits down at the table
across from where I'm eating dinner.

"So, why do you hate me?"

He sounds genuinely hurt, and I realize
how childish I've been acting . . .
being mean to a boy to get him to like me,
like a little kid shoving her crush in the sandbox.

I accuse him of being a tease to all the girls,
and his response makes my heart beat faster.

"The only girl I actually want
to flirt with here won't
give me the time of day

unless I corner her while
she's stealing cookies."

I don't know how to react so I roll my eyes
as he moves closer and leans against the wall.

"I even saved her life once. Jumped in front of a bullet for her."

A BOW ON TOP

At the end of the summer,
Grant and I go for one last hike together, and
it starts to pour just as we're nearing the top
of the Palisades.

Thunder and lightning and mud and fog
land us beneath an apocalyptic sky.

We're not sure whether it's worth carrying on . . .

and then, suddenly, the gloom disperses,
clearing to majestic wisps of cloud
below the peak, and
the longest, fullest rainbow
I've ever seen in real life
stretches directly overhead.

I'm standing under the colored arch of mist,
hand in hand with a guy who reminds me
that relationships can be easy
and simple
and normal.

THE BEGINNING OF THE END: SENIOR YEAR

It's the first party of senior year.
I haven't seen you,
or even talked to you,
in three months.

You stand in the doorway with a beer;
I'm sitting on the couch.

As soon as our eyes meet,
I get up and step over all
the legs to get to you.

You meet me in the middle of the room.

We stare into each other's eyes a moment
before hugging, and I feel
suddenly
like a different person—
the person I had missed being all summer with Grant.

"Hi, Maxwell," I whisper as we embrace,
and it hurts so good to remember all over again
how perfectly we seem to fit in each other's arms.

"Hi, Daltwell."

Joanna joins us as we reminisce about
all the silly things that happened abroad,
and as the three of us stand there,
drinking and laughing,

I feel pangs of nostalgia for when
we were all best friends.

Then Frank Ocean's "Super Rich Kids"
bumps over the speakers.

I slink to the beat,
leading you with my eyes
to an open space in the crowd.

We dance and laugh
and dance some more,
just like the old days.

The next morning, we wake up
together and spend
the day showing each other
new music and funny videos
and rolling around in bed.

You're kissing my torso,
and we're both giggling
as you reacquaint yourself
with the three moles speckling
my stomach and ribs.
You used to refer to them
as the Jonas Brothers,
and now you're renaming
them Harry, Ron, and
Bilbo Baggins.

When I tell you how
I always used to want

to get those moles removed,
you cluck in disapproval
because you love them
in a way that makes me
like them, and nothing
can touch this
perfect moment

until

you catch a glimpse of my phone—
the background of me and Grant—
and you grow quiet,
and minutes later,
you're gathering up your things.

ROYAL BALLS

The truth is
I haven't even spoken to Grant
on the phone since I left the ranch
a month and a half ago,
and as I drive to the airport late
on a Friday night to pick him up,
I feel the same old nervous jitters setting in again—
the ones that make me feel
like I'm disguising myself
as a female stereotype,
passive and delicate.

But it's exciting.

Joanna and Sophie buy a bunch of liquor and beer,
move my speakers
from my room to the back porch of our house,
and invite all of our friends over.

I sit on the kitchen counter drinking Coronas;
Grant stands next to me, making conversation
with Theo and Paul about being from the South . . .

Meanwhile, you're all

                                                               alone

in the big house on Dub Street,
losing your mind, feeling
like all of your friends have gone

                                        off to the royal ball

                                        and left you

in a sullen pile
of shattered glass slippers
and spliff ash.

TO KILL CHIVALRY

All weekend Grant is such a gentleman—
holding doors for me,
pulling my chair out at dinner,
and carrying my backpack on a hike near campus.

But the more chivalrous he is,
the more I long for

shoe-shopping in Europe with you,
or binge-watching episodes of *The Bachelor*,
or you accidentally slamming a door in my face
and then laughing at my scowl.

And the truth is,
it's almost a relief,
two days later,
when I drive Grant back
to the Burlington airport
for his flight home.

ON THE DRIVE BACK FROM THE AIRPORT

It's dark.
It's been raining all day,
and my mind is ready to curl up
and disappear into sleep.

I think about reaching out to you,
if only to apologize for the party
you felt you needed to avoid.

About halfway to campus, I descend
a back-road mountain pass,
the drowsy fog clouding my thoughts,
and it feels like my car is floating.

And suddenly the car fishtails,
swerving back and forth, like
a bottle revving up for the spin
at a middle school make-out party.

I panic and stomp on the brakes.
The tail end whips forward.
The tires lift off the road,
and the car flips clockwise
over the passenger side,
tumbling twice down the decline,
landing right-side-up
perpendicular to the road
on the inner shoulder
closest to the mountain.

In those elongated seconds, I feel
like I'm bent backwards, hovering
beneath a limbo stick—
unsure whether
I'm about to fall.

I'm facing the steep incline of the mountain.
A loud whirring of white noise
emanates from the static radio,
its buzz filling the empty silence.

All the lights are on inside the car,
illuminating the sparkling, granular crumbles
of tempered glass that litter the floors and seats.

The windshield is smashed in,
ripped from the seal at the top,
pushing the rearview mirror
down toward the center console.

A Macintosh-scented car freshener
that my dad got me for Christmas
dangles just over the gear shift.

My seat belt is tight across my body.

Then all at once, the rest of my being
comes crashing into real time.
The searing memory of what just occurred
jolts through my mind in a rush of adrenaline.

Feeling more awake than I have in months,
I look around at the crumpled windshield,

the concave roof, the missing mirrors,
the broken glass everywhere,
and understand that I really am still here,
still living in the middle of it all,
without even one tiny scratch.

I click the seat belt loose
and turn around to survey
the back seat, also glittering
in granular glass.

I sit in the car, processing the scene,
the odd sight of the keys still in the ignition,
the gear shift still in drive, and
the glowing blue dashboard screen
still showing the current station,
as if I can just hit the gas again
and continue driving.

And then I'm shaking like
I'm about to erupt,
and I don't feel real
even though I know I must be,
and the most unsettling part is
the mere sight of these things,
being able to believe in them,
realizing that they would
still be here to be seen
even if I
wasn't
here

to see them.

BACK AT THE HOUSE

The girls sit with me
in the living room
as I relive the accident.

The front door flies open and

it's you—
scanning the room
with a look of desperation
on your face.

I burst into tears—
the kind of crying
I do when
I hear my mother's voice
on the phone and
lose all composure.

You kneel in front of me.
We hug for a long time
before you lean back and
look me up and down,
still holding my hands.

You reach up with your sleeve
to wipe the tears from my cheeks.

Moments later, we're under
the covers in my bed.

You hold me close to you.
You rub my back as I
fall asleep in your arms.

I don't even tell Grant
about the car accident.

It goes without saying
that there will not be
another visit.

TURN UP

We're at the Hannaford supermarket
to buy vodka and whiskey.
On our way out,
we pass the vegetable aisle
and get an idea.

Later that night, at a party
in the Atwater senior suites,
we're shouting,

"TURN UP!"

as loud as we can
and throwing
fresh turnips
at all the freshmen.

DRUNK DIALING

When I answer your 2 a.m. phone call,
your voice is fuzzy with booze,
and there's a lot of shouting
and music in the background.

"I'm with Leopold. Come to Dub.
We want you to come smoke with us!"

"Leopold?"

We know only one Leopold,
and I'm almost positive you're joking.

You lower your voice.

"Yes. Leopold. Em, I think he wants
to hook up with us. Or you. Or us!"

LEOPOLD TOWNSEND?!

As in, the international student from Sweden in our year,
arguably one of the hottest guys at school,
causing girls—and guys—from all four grades
to sigh with lust as he passes by?!

As in, perfect blond hair that falls just right at every angle,
tall, broad stature, measuring in at about 6'2" and 180 pounds,
piercing deep-blue eyes, lightly tanned, smooth complexion,
and, of course, that exotic Scandinavian accent?!

I do *not* believe you.

THEN YOU PUT HIM ON THE PHONE

and I get out of my warm bed,
back into my clothes,
and start the twenty-minute
walk to Dub Street.

I find you, Theo,
and the one and only
Leopold Townsend
sitting in the living room,
a haze of smoke hanging
in the air and cans of beer
in each of your hands.

My heart is still pounding, and
my breath is short as I crack open a beer.

"All right, well, unless y'all
need me to chaperone here . . ."
Theo smirks as he backs into the hallway.
"I bid you good night!"

The three of us—
you, Leopold, and I—
drink and listen to music
in awkward anticipation
of what is about to happen.

You and I lead by example,
stripping down to our underwear
and kissing as Leopold watches us
in a drunken daze, telling us

how sexy we are together,
how beautiful and blond.

The lights in your room are all still on,
and then I'm on all fours in my thong
between Leopold's thick, long legs.

His left palm rests on the back of my head,
and he's groaning a little, eyes closed,
while you rest your head on his chest.

He doesn't seem interested in kissing you,
and the next thing I know you're lying
on the other side of the bed,
just watching.

In the morning,
we wake up in your bed,
just the two of us,
and shriek with laughter
as we try to piece together
the epic failure that was our first threesome.

The story bounces around our social circles
and you and I feel reinvigorated,
realizing the answer to our problems
might be as simple as
hooking up with other people
together.

THE SECOND THIRD

We don't expect to find another third
on our small campus in the month
we have left of our senior year,
but a few weeks after our night
with Leopold, we meet Mason Hewitt.

We're at a party, and Mason is not
shy about making it clear
that he finds the two of us
very intriguing, very beautiful.

So we go back to your room.
The lights are off.

You and I get fully naked
before we help Mason out of his clothes
and into the bed between us.

At first, you're both ravishing me,
but then you get a little more adventurous
with each other,
and in another life,
I'd probably be so into this, but
right here, right now,
I feel very unsure of
what to do with myself
while the two of you
crawl all over each other.

I slip out of the bed,
wrap a blanket around
my naked body, and
huff out of the room.

After a little while, you emerge,
wrapped in a blanket of your own,
and find me on the orange velvet couch
in the dark of the living room.

You sit down next to me.
Your eyes are searching mine
for some kind of allowance.

A few minutes later, you're gone, and
the reality sets in, and I want
to shrink into a speck and float away.

As I lie on the couch
in the dark living room,
staring at the wall,
I try as hard as I can
to focus my attention
on the sound of a little black fly
buzzing against the windows.

If I can just concentrate
on the fly, it will drown out the noise
from your room down the hall.

But as I listen to the soft buzzing,
a fleeting question rises to the surface of
my consciousness—

How has this become my life?

The next night,
when I ask you
how it was,
your answer
breaks my
already-broken
heart:

"It all just felt really . . .

normal."

AT LAST

We decide to stay together
as a couple
for the last week of college.

The night before graduation,
when all the seniors gather
on the football field at 5 a.m.
to watch the sunrise,
no one seems to know
where you are, and your phone
keeps going to voicemail.

As the sky turns from a deep, dark blue to light gray,
I make my way over to Dub Street, heart pounding
and head spinning,
dreading that you're either dead in a ditch or
in bed with a guy.

I crack open the front door
and then pause, because sometimes,
when something really terrible is happening,
I can shake my head back and forth
hard enough to wake myself up.

But this time
I can't shake the sight
of Mason's

faded
     red

        sneakers

in the hallway.

GRADUATION DAY

The first person to swim from Cuba
to Florida without a shark cage
gives a very moving and empowering
commencement address at graduation
this morning.

I'm sitting here in my black robe
next to the other English majors
watching her mouth move,

but I don't hear any of it

and

behind my sunglasses
there are tears in my eyes.

ENDING

I arrive home a college graduate.
I start the miserable process
of unpacking the car,
and it feels like I just
finished watching a long,
dramatic film—
the kind that has an unsettling,
unsatisfying ending

that leaves you feeling

empty.

At the bottom of a suitcase,
I come upon an unfamiliar
orange manila envelope.

Across the back of it,
written in black marker,
there's a note.

It's addressed to: *Babe My Babe.*

Your messy, swirly handwriting.

The note says that despite your actions, you hope I know
there's no part of you that doesn't love me.
That even though it hurts, we are worth it.
That no one makes you feel the way I do.

That you've been loving me for way too long to ever stop.

Love,
Max (Babe Your Babe)

I sit down on the driveway and cry
tears that look like raindrops
when they hit the asphalt.

Soon I'm wailing, and
an image of you
watching me ugly-cry
on the pavement
flashes through my mind,
and I start to laugh.

I'm laughing and crying amid
a pile of bedding-stuffed garbage bags.

And now I'm not so sure
that this is the end.

RELOCATING

You get a job at a school
for teenagers with special needs
in New York City.

A month after that,
I get a job at a hip
young ad agency in the East Village,
and now I'm moving to New York, too.

We settle into separate apartments in Brooklyn.
You in Bushwick, me in Gowanus.

I don't know how or why, but
the future we've always joked about—
how you'd be a teacher and stay-at-home dad
and I'd be a breadwinning business mom—
is beginning to align, as if
the universe is laughing at our joke
as it rearranges our postgrad constellations.

An urban relocation of Max and Emily World.

We're living in the real world,
the adult world, but still acting
like our college selves.

I stare out the window of my apartment,
my gaze resting on the fluorescent red clock
of the Williamsburgh Savings Bank Tower.

With its tapered obelisk
thrusting high and its dome top,
this is the very structure that prompted
the "World's Most Phallic Building" contest in 2003.

All evening, we've been fighting
about our relationship status.
Laughing softly to myself,
I turn to look at you.

"Do you ever feel like your whole life
is just one big dick joke?"

KEVIN

The leaves on the potted trees
are turning the same colors
as they do up north in Vermont,
but there's something misplaced
about autumn foliage in New York City.

As the era of dating apps dawns upon us,
our relationship hinges on which one of us
will find an interest in someone new first.

We set our profiles to both genders,
swiping through males and females alike.

I match with a boy named Kevin.
He's a year older and works
a variety of freelance jobs in film.

The physical chemistry is there,
and we share enough interests
to make it worth more than a few dates.

Maybe Kevin will be the one
who can help me see the light,
help me believe in anything other
than you.

I avoid bringing him along with me
to parties and make sure you're not
there before inviting him to come.

I see you every now and then . . .
I ask you whether you'll meet Kevin,
but you have absolutely no desire to.

The last thing you say to me
before we stop talking
isn't exactly *to* me
because it's a note you leave
on my computer that
refers to me in the third person.

You write that you're realizing Emily
has been searching for something more all along.
She's been searching for art. And you have, too.
You just thought you'd found it already.

In Emily.

She was your art.
You were never Emily's art.
You were always her disaster.

ABOVE ALL

Ramona and Sophie throw a party
at their apartment in Williamsburg.

I stand at their kitchen counter,
mixing whiskey and ginger ale,
when Sophie mentions something I
haven't yet heard about you.

"He's going to Australia for the summer?"
I sip my drink and try to act casual.

The smell of marijuana
wafts from the fire escape,
and I follow it out the window.

At the other end of the grated platform,
standing in a small circle of friends,
there you are.

A few moments pass before we make eye contact,
and when we do, I stealthily flash my personal spliff,
and you make your way over to me.

You're not exactly smiling, but
you're not frowning, either.

"Hey."

Your distant, cordial tone
makes my heart hurt.

Gesturing to my hand, you hold up a lighter.
You point up the metal rungs that lead to the roof.

I wonder why we haven't spoken in such a long time.

You start up the ladder, never looking down
before you disappear over the parapet.
I tuck the spliff into my bra and follow.

I find you sitting on a low divider wall
on the other side of the roof,
gazing at the faded contours of the sunset.

You tell me that your flight is on Wednesday at 4 a.m.

"A long one, isn't it?" I say.

You tip your head to the side
and exhale a puff of smoke.

"That's what *he* said," you joke.
"Oh, it's what he said, now?" I reply,
and you give me a sarcastic, unenthused look.

We talk about what we've been listening to lately.
I play you a few songs from my phone.

We laugh, and I study your face—
the scruff of your dirty blond beard,
your long, dark eyelashes,
and your thick, unruly eyebrows.
I reach up and feel the hairs
in between your brows with one finger.

You ask about my family.

I pick at my cuticles as I fill you in.
You notice the old habit and
gently pull my hand away from the other.

Before letting go, you squeeze it,
and we look into each other's eyes.

For a moment, I'm back in sophomore year,
standing across from you at the pong table,
realizing how stupid I've been
for denying my love for you.

The spliff is gone, and the sounds
from the party below are getting
a bit louder as more people arrive.

"You're going to be safe while you're there,
right, Max?" I ask.

I can see your mind working.
The thoughts and feelings floating
in the air between us seem too raveled to pin down.
But I encourage you to try anyway.
I can't help myself.

"Nothing is not worth saying to me
if you want to say it."

"It's just a shitty and fucked-up
but beautiful feeling, Em," you say.
"It's like the whole world stops

or disappears
when I'm up on this roof with you,
and it's just the two of us . . .
and I just want to live up here
like this
with you
forever,
in our world together.
And it's sad
because I also know
that when we go back down that ladder,
we'll no longer be in our world,
up here
where it's just you and me
and nothing else matters."

Your words summon all of the history between us.
Tears reflect in our eyes as we stare at one another,
and I wish I could wrap my arms around you
and press my face under your jaw,
where I know it fits so perfectly.

I hug you, and you hold me tight.
"You know I feel the same way, Max."
Your shoulders bounce lightly as you weep.

When we let go, you shake your arms out
like you're shaking off the emotions.
Then you head for the ladder.

I sit motionless for another moment
before following you across the roof.

Standing on the top rungs of the ladder,
you turn around—
not so much to face me
as to begin your descent—
but our eyes meet
for one more aching moment.

Then you drop your gaze

and disappear.

SUNFLOWERS

When you return to New York in the fall,
I've broken up
with Kevin.

Who was I kidding?
It was never over between us.
And now we've found our way back to each other.

We take turns feeling spiteful
and jealous or hopelessly in love.

One night in the first week of December
you come over with a bouquet of sunflowers,
and the thick, scratchy stalks bristle in my hands
as I stick them in a jar of water.

Indelicate as they are,
you've never given me flowers before.

It's a sweet, pleasant surprise,
yet here we are, still—
almost five years later—
chasing after the ghost
of an apocalyptic horse,
trying to bring it back to life
just so we can continue beating it to death.

As I place the sunflowers on the windowsill,
a few of the garish heads smile up at me
in blameless delight.

The rest hang heavy.

AFTER NEW YEAR'S

I sit in my bed in Gowanus
with tears streaming down my cheeks,
leaving dark splotches on my sweatshirt
as I read the email you've sent me.

After every "I love you," there is a "but."

You don't want it to be possible
for a guy to make you as happy as I do.
You never want to lose touch
with me or not know about my life.

And if we don't end up together,
you are always going to imagine
what your life would have been like with me.
And you know it would be amazing,
and you know I would make you happy.

After reading your note,
a hundred clichés about broken hearts hang
from my neck like sandbags.

I call in sick to work.
I go in to work stoned.
I have no motivation
to wake up in the morning,
get dressed, eat food.

You have a permanent hold on my heart . . .
like a giant red metronome ticking off the beat.

In a fit of tears, I grab the wilting sunflowers
from their jar and throw them out the window
into the dumpster on the sidewalk.

The next morning, I perch on the sill to smoke
and glance down to find, on the fire escape below mine,
the sunflowers I tossed the night before
slumped over the edge, just out of reach.

All through the winter, I watch
as the rotting blooms
shrivel and freeze.

ON A BENCH ON THE WEST SIDE

There's a big, dumb inflatable dolphin
bobbing over the pink baby waves
of the Hudson. I keep staring at it
while you protest my idea
to cut all communication for a while.

It's hard to focus on a single thought,
so instead my mind starts playing out
my hypothetical escape:
I jump into the water,
mount the dolphin,
and sail off majestically
toward the horizon . . .

As the sun goes down in front of us,
the sky constantly evolving
and changing colors in this
picture-perfect breakup ambiance,
you agree to give me space,
just the six weeks I've asked for.

We hug goodbye, and now
I'm lingering here for hours.

It's so beautiful—
the changing sky
and its filmlike reflection in the water—
that I can't turn away.

So I stay even after
all has gone dark

and the watery pictures have stilled
and vanished.

I stay because
I need to be sure
it isn't going to get pretty again.

REACHING

I've waited until late April
to finally contact you.

I call you, but your phone
goes to voicemail.

So I wait another few days and try again.
Still, no response.

I try to reassure myself that
no matter what is going on,
I can handle it, but
I can't shake the feeling
that something terrible has happened
during our break from each other.

Finally, you text me to say you're sorry
for missing my calls and that
you're fine, just busy.

Your response seems oddly formal and robotic . . .

I can't restrain myself. Instead of texting back,
I call.

After a few rings,
you answer, and
your voice sounds generic,
like it could be any male voice
in the world.

"Hi."

I try not to sound indignant.

"Is everything okay with you?
Oh . . . I mean, if you're busy right now,
that's fine; I just—
Yeah, I'm all right . . .

I'm sorry, but why does this feel
so weird right now, Max?"

"I'm not sure if you already knew this

or not,

but

I'm kind of dating someone."

And just like that,
we
aren't
"we"
anymore.

And you

are just

another "him."

REFLECTIONS: CHILDHOOD NIGHTMARE

I couldn't have been any older
than five or six:

It's my dad and me,
and we're standing outside
some sort of military base
in the middle of the desert.

And there's warfare going on all around us,
bombs dropping and guns and fighting.

I look up to my dad,
and he's dressed in an army uniform . . .
and I'm pulling on his arm,
trying to get him to look down at me.

I'm saying, *"Dad! Dad, come on!*
We have to get out of here!"

He looks down at me,
but he doesn't know who I am.

He doesn't know I'm his daughter,
and he brushes me away.

Eventually,
I realize that
it's time to wake up.

MAX'S NEW BOYFRIEND

"I love your hair! Is that natural?"

Up until now, I've only ever seen
a few photos of Shane on social media,
and in all of them he has a big,
eye-crinkling grin on his face.

Standing in front of me
in the kitchen of Sophie and Ramona's apartment,
complimenting my curls,
Shane is a real human, lifelike and animated,
and I'm oddly thrown off
by how similar he and Max look,
almost like they could be brothers.

Same height, same soft, round features,
same short hairstyle and scruff.
The only major differences are hair and eye color;
Shane's dark brown hair and eyes contrast
next to Max's blond and blue.

Max mixes drinks for himself and Shane
as the three of us stand near the fridge
talking about my hair.

"I hated it all through high school and college.
It was always just this big nest of knots.
I had no idea how to handle it,
so I'd just straighten it every day."

My brain goes into some kind of autopilot survival mode.
I avoid eye contact with Max.

"Anyway, it was pretty exhausting," I continue,
"trying to make it straight all those years.
Some things you just can't force straight,
am I right?"

I excuse myself abruptly and hurry away,
flinging myself into the bathroom.
Staring into the mirror over the sink,
I smile at my reflection,
then burst into a drunken fit of giggles,
and it feels oddly thrilling
to have a moment like this
alone with myself.

I down the rest of my whiskey ginger
and then rejoin the party,
steering clear of Max and Shane.

As the night goes on and everyone gets drunker,
I inevitably bump into the two of them again
on the fire escape.

With more liquor in our systems,
we talk cheerfully and laugh,
and as I get to know Shane better,
I slowly begin to grapple
with a disconcerting truth—

I like him.

I can see how he's a suitable match for Max.

They have the same taste in music,
they dress similarly, they seem
to have a calm, drama-free way
of communicating with each other,
and Shane also dated girls in high school
and didn't fully come out until college.

"He also likes to write, just like you, Em!" Max says.
"He's written and directed a few plays.
I've read them; they're really good.
You would like them."

REFLECTIONS: FIFTH BOYFRIEND

Berlin.
The beginning of November.
Semester abroad.

I lean against the railing
of Max's balcony
with my eyes closed,
letting the late-morning sun caress me
instead of cuddling in close to him.

He kisses my jaw and
wraps his arm around me.

"Your poor fingers," he says.

Max knows all about my terrible habit
of picking at the skin around my cuticles.

I like to peel it back slowly
and then watch
as a thin strip of fresh blood
oozes
from the raw underlayer of skin.

Those close to me can gauge my stress level
by the number of bandages I have
wrapped around the tips of my fingers.

Max coos into my ear as he kisses each finger
and then holds my hand, and I can feel butterflies
shaking out their dampened wings inside my stomach.

He's so good at holding me accountable,
knocking my hands apart,
begging me to stop mutilating my skin.

As the sunlight dims behind a low-hanging cloud,
he brings my face close to his and asks,

"Dear fräulein, why do you do this to yourself?"

as if he doesn't already know.

POETRY IN MOTION

It's well past midnight when I leave the party
at Sophie and Ramona's—
leave Max and Shane—
and step onto an empty subway car
at the 2nd Avenue F station.

No one gets on at Delancey/Essex.
No one at East Broadway.

I'm drunk and alone when one of those
"Poetry in Motion" placards catches my eye
in the corner of the car—

"A Strange Beautiful Woman"
by Marilyn Nelson

—eight short lines
about meeting a strange
beautiful woman
in the mirror.

Hey,

the speaker and her reflection
both ask,

What you doing here?

I stand in front of the placard,
reading the poem

over and over again
until I enter a sort of trance.

The music in my headphones is on shuffle,
and that song "Dance Yrself Clean" by LCD Soundsystem
comes on. Slowly, I close my eyes
and let the beat move me.

DECISIONS

In the morning, slices of white sunlight
sneak between the blinds,

and outside, someone lays on their horn,
producing a sound like the dramatic fermata
at the end of a song.

I know that last night
I unearthed a fear I'd
buried deep
five years ago
in a stairwell in Milliken:

my fear of falling in love
and losing it all.

And now,
having fallen and lost,
I have to decide what to do—*who to be*—
in response.

Max and I will never be
Max and Emily
again.

But can Emily be Emily again?

The honking quiets.

I stare
at the cross sections of light

glowing in the far corner
of the ceiling and begin
to coax myself
up.

ACCOUNTABILITY

I quit my job and leave the city.

I go back to rural northern Connecticut
where I grew up,
where the night sky is impossibly dark
and the roads are so empty and silent.

I've stopped smoking, so the nights
in particular have become
long-lost sober reminders
of an entirely separate existence.

I miss the comforting glow and buzz of the city,
but I'm coming to appreciate the bright stars
I had forgotten existed,
and the distant hoot of an owl
interrupting the soft hum of crickets,
and the sound of the trees inhaling
and exhaling a sudden gust of wind.

I'm learning how to chop firewood with my dad;
I go on long walks through the woods with my mom;
I smash rocks apart on the driveway with my niece and nephew.

My dreams are shockingly elaborate and vivid,
like the constellations I'm rediscovering.

Sometimes, I dream about Max,
and other times, I dream about drugs.

But for the most part, I keep having this dream
about rising high in the air above everything
and floating over it all to where I need to go.

In these dreams, it takes concerted focus
for me to rise up.

The moment I lose concentration,
gravity pulls my body closer and closer to the ground.

I'm like Uncle Albert in *Mary Poppins*,
or Charlie and Grandpa Joe in *Charlie and the Chocolate Factory*,
or Wendy and the kids in *Peter Pan*.

Only, instead of laughter or burps or fairy dust,
I seem to be relying on
my own resolve.

FORGING

A family friend—a blacksmith—
needs help in his shop,
and I need a job,
so every morning for the next few months,
I don heavy Carhartts and steel-toed boots
and drive to town.

I learn how to weld metals together
and heat iron in the forge;
how to work the massive power hammers
and the drill press and the loud, groaning band saw;
how to spark, light, and adjust the butane valve on the blowtorch;
how to grind and sharpen the blade on a knife;
and how to read the color and the grain of the metal
for thickness and density and strength.

And in the evenings, I write.

It's not cold enough yet for a fire,
but I build one in the living room fireplace anyway.
The sound and movement of the flames,
like tiny, pale flags whipping in an invisible wind,
make me feel less alone with my words.

My fingers swollen from work,
I type at my desk
with little aim
but to make something

anything

new.

FIELD NOTES

It's one of those freakishly warm days
in the middle of February
when you have to pause for a moment
to process what you're feeling against your skin.

All winter long, when chunks of icy snow
scraped from frozen windshields
melted in my boots
or the air was so brutally cold
that it was impossible to think straight,
I pined for a day like this—
bright sun and warm air,
stepping outdoors
and hardly noticing
a change in temperature.

In a flannel shirt, jeans, and a winter hat,
I feel heavily overdressed
and sweaty after fifteen minutes of
walking through the woods.

I cross the brook behind the house
on dark, slick stones,
then head up the leaf-covered hill
to where the woods open up
into a huge field.

As I stand at its edge,
I can feel my body remembering how to function
in the warmth.

As I walk the perimeter of the field,
I wonder what Max is doing—
where he is, whom he's with,
whether he's happy.

Words from the letter he wrote to me
a year ago come to mind.

I never want to lose touch
or not know what's going on
in each other's lives.

Yet here we are.

Here I am.

REFLECTIONS: THE LAST TIME I SAW MAX

I'm sitting on a bench in Washington Square Park.

It's the end of September,
but it's warm, and a bunch of young guys
are splashing around in the big fountain near the Arch;
little kids are blowing bubbles
and dancing around with their nannies;
college students are sprawled across colorful blankets
in the patches of grass,
holding books above their faces
or napping on each other.

Max is quiet as he sits down next to me.
He seems to understand that I'm having a moment.

We watch as an old man and an old lady
take their time standing up from a bench across from us,
gathering their hats and canes
and situating themselves to continue walking.

We watch as a young muscular man rollerblades by,
wearing nothing but a bikini top and ripped jean shorts,
blasting techno music from speakers in his backpack.

Without turning to me, Max breaks the silence.

"So . . . what are you going to be for Halloween?"

The old icebreaker sits between us for a moment.

"Don't think I'll be dressing up this year," I reply.

He knows I'm leaving the city to write
and brings up Shane's writing,
telling me again
how much I would like it.

I ask him what Shane thinks
of our past together.

"I don't know. I think he sees it as
part of my extended coming-out story."

His words feel painfully dismissive,
as though he's saying our entire relationship
was a mistake.

I finally turn to look at him.

"Is that what you think we were?"

He swallows and breathes in,
and when he finally speaks,
I can hear the pain in his voice.

"Shane just doesn't understand, Em.
He doesn't know what it was like
for me to be in love
with a woman
for so long."

Even though Max is wearing sunglasses,
I can see that tears are forming in his eyes.

And at last, I can see that
I don't need him
to tell me what we were
because I already know.

We were the joke
that made us laugh until we cried.

Valentine's Day diapers,
black bean burgers,
and turnips thrown at freshmen;
Halloween dares, late night spliffs,
and poorly planned threesomes;
a fair fight with Ponyboy,
a journal entry to God,
and a little black fly
buzzing in my ear.

We were slamming doors
and breaking promises;
we were experimenting and dreaming
and trusting the unknown.

We were in Max and Emily World
learning about life and love and
teaching each other
how to become ourselves.

We were a mistake.

And some of the most beautiful
things in life come
from mistakes.

FIELD NOTES, CONTINUED

At the far corner of the field,
near the foundation of a house that burned down years ago,
I pause for a moment to face the February sky
and soak in the sunlight.

I sit on a pile of crumbling brick
that was once a hearth.

As the shadows grow longer
in the late-afternoon sun,
more words from Max's letter
blaze through my mind.

If we don't end up together,
I am always going to imagine
what my life would have been like with you.
I know it would be amazing;
I know you would make me happy.

I don't know where Max is,
or whom he is with,
or whether he's happy.

I have no idea what our life would be like
if we were together; maybe it would be amazing
and we'd make each other happy,
but it's just as likely that it would be disastrous
and we'd make each other miserable.

I suppose finding a soul mate really can go either way.

Before rising again to carry on
through the dead grass and melting snow,
I shed a layer of flannel and pull off my hat.

Then I stand up and turn around
to take in the full panoramic view.

Alone in this field
I'm struck by the notion that this is my place
in time and space.

It's as though I've been here all along
waiting for myself.

Hey, what you doing here?

SURPRISE BEGINNING

As spring arrives to thaw the ground
and awaken dormant roots,
my aimless drafting
starts to feel less aimless.

I think back to my last days on the campus
where this story began

and watch an archived YouTube video
of the commencement address Diana Nyad gave
at my graduation from Middlebury.

Much to my surprise, she ends her speech
by quoting the final lines of "The Summer Day"
by Mary Oliver:

> *Tell me,*

Oliver begins,

And what follows is a question that,
in its directness,
begs a vulnerability
and a self-confidence
that, until now,
have eluded me.

Like an echo through the darkness,
the question lingers,

waiting . . .

And for the first time,
I'm not looking to someone else
for the answer.

ACKNOWLEDGMENTS

Thank you to Jay Parini, for teaching me why poetry matters and how to write about what I care about; to Connor Eck, for believing in my story, even in its roughest of drafts, and for guiding me through it when I couldn't find my way alone; and to Melissa Rhodes Zahorsky, for reading, understanding, and then expertly refining *Be Straight with Me.*

Thank you to my family, for loving me even when I am hard to love: to Dad, for gifting me with my first and most magical memories of storytelling; to Mom, for allowing me the space and freedom to turn my mistakes into something beautiful; to Dooey, for pushing me to be realistic and challenging me to succeed; to Amy, for being my first real reader and my most valuable critic; to Auds and Ev, for reminding me to look for the beauty and excitement in everyday life; and to Gee, for seeing me, hearing me, protecting me, and inspiring me since page one.

And
thank you
to you,
who I called "Max"
in this book,
for being
straight with me
when I couldn't
be straight with myself.

Enjoy *Be Straight with Me* as an audiobook, wherever audiobooks are sold.